"Sharon Risher is the very definition of a hero: s.
pain and turned it into activism in an effort to prevent other families
from experiencing the same anguish her family has. Sharon's passion
shines through on every page, and her compelling story shows us all
how to find courage and compassion in even the darkest tragedy. I've
been honored to work side by side with Sharon since 2015, and I'm so
grateful for her guidance and wisdom—in real life, and in her book."
— Shannon Watts, founder of Moms Demand Action for Gun Sense
in America

"*For Such a Time as This* is a beautiful but bittersweet memoir of a
woman of God facing the loss of her beloved family by gun violence.
Rev. Risher is truly one who has been called to rise in faith as a conduit
for love, acceptance, and forgiveness. Her story will forever stand
as truth and compassion in America's shameful culture of hate and
discrimination played out through gun violence."
— Rep. Lucy McBath, Sixth Congressional District of Georgia

"When you read Rev. Sharon Risher's phenomenal life story, you will
want to hug her, cry with her, laugh with her. She sweeps you up with
her unstoppable spirit. Faith keeps her resilient in the face of tragedy,
the unthinkable murder of her mother at a prayer meeting in church.
She inspires you to overcome colossal hurdles and face life with gusto
and humor...and forgiveness."
— Abigail Pesta, award-winning journalist, author of *The Girls*,
coauthor of *How Dare the Sun Rise*

"Rev. Sharon Risher has inspired countless Americans with her journey
from gun violence survivor to activist. With such moving honesty
and raw emotion, hers is a story of resilience in the face of hatred and
violence. This book will touch your heart and make you want to stand
with her in the movement to end gun violence."
— Christopher Kocher, director of Everytown Survivor Network

"In *For Such a Time as This,* Rev. Sharon Risher writes in a voice that those who know her will recognize, the authentic one of an imperfect preacher who smokes and cusses and fought addiction, and who brings to ministry the lessons lived in a real life. That includes her honest account of a long and painful journey, often at the brunt of other people's judgments, to forgive the white supremacist who murdered her mother and eight others inside Emanuel AME Church.

No family is perfect, and Risher describes how her mother's violent death ripped at the fabric of hers, already torn by the loss of one sister just two years before the massacre and another sister two years after. There are lessons for us all in her story, including an important plea for America to confront the twin evils of racism and gun violence, as she is doing in her new life's role as an 'accidental activist.' That she has heeded this important calling amid such suffering is an inspiration for all of us to read her story and then go do our part."

— Jennifer Berry Hawes, author of *Grace Will Lead Us Home*

"I consider myself incredibly lucky to count Sharon Risher as a dear friend. Reading these stories she's told me in person evokes the same tears and the same impossible laughter that we've shared. Her authentic presence, embodying the defiant joy of our common human experience as only the utterly heartbroken can do, shines forth in *For Such a Time as This: Hope and Forgiveness after the Charleston Massacre* as the next best thing to being with her in person. As someone who once espoused the same toxic cowardice and irresponsibility that twisted the weak mind of the suffering fool who murdered Ethel Lance and eight other wonderful souls, I say with authority that Sharon Risher's profound voice is righteous kryptonite to the fear and ignorance that compose hate. The faith in humanity that this book inspires ensures that hate will never win in the hearts of those who read it."

— Arno Arr Michaelis IV, speaker, author, educator, filmmaker, and former white supremacist

"When we look at the staggering statistics around gun violence in America, we never know the stories of the surviving loved ones. *For Such a Time as This* is one story of one brave woman, but it's a book that can change hearts and minds. Rev. Sharon Risher's honest, wrenching memoir about her journey since her mother's murder at Mother Emanuel Church during the summer of 2015 is nothing short of inspirational. Guided by her faith, Rev. Risher has become a national spokesperson for gun control. This redemptive story reminds us of the power inside each and every one of us to stand up for what is right and make a better world for all of us."

> — Marjory Wentworth coauthor of *We Are Charleston, Tragedy and Triumph at Mother Emanuel*

"Rev. Sharon Risher is not one to be timid in the face of injustice, suffering, or controversy. Out of the anguish of her own unspeakable loss after her mother and cousins were gunned down in a church basement by an unapologetic white supremacist, she takes us on the journey no one wants to go on. Her training as a minister and chaplain helps us understand the complex emotions that tormented her in the aftermath of such personal tragedy. In this 'can't-put-it-down' page-turner, the author doesn't mince words in conveying what it means to work through such pain, anger, isolation, and fear. Yet, in the end, she generously shares the hopeful lessons she learned so we can vicariously benefit from them. It takes extraordinary bravery to do what Sharon Risher has done by so candidly sharing her story—and we should all be grateful to God and to her for it! This book is a gift to humankind."

> — Rob Schenck, author of *Costly Grace: An Evangelical Minister's Rediscovery of Faith, Hope and Love* and subject of Abigail Disney's Emmy Award-winning documentary, *The Armor of Light*

"To read this book is to be challenged to become a better, more aware, and empathic person. Rev. Risher begins with the story of her mother's tragic death then takes deep dives into topics like growing up black, the messy realities of family, gun violence, politics, and more. The reader is in skilled hands with Rev. Risher, who has served as chaplain, pastor, mother, and activist. In sharing her own heart and mind she encourages us to think more deeply and to be more painfully and uncomfortably honest as we consider difficult topics like grief, the death penalty, race, faith, and forgiveness. Rev. Risher isn't about simple answers or clichés. She is, instead, about the gritty and complex realities that confront survivors of gun violence, the black community, and real-life families. Reading this book made me feel both understood and challenged. It opened my eyes, informed me in important ways, and challenged me to think through how I might live in more authentic and grace-giving ways. I finished it wanting to hear more from this inspired and honest writer. Her brave vulnerability was permission-giving in important ways. I felt that my flawed humanity was affirmed and welcomed and yet I also found myself inspired to reach just a bit farther in my pursuits to make the world a better place. Rev. Risher's determination to remember the nine lives lost in Charleston (and countless others across the country) as well as her willingness to offer up her own experiences as instructions for how to live through trauma is inspirational. I will be waiting, excitedly, for more from this incredible and talented woman!"
— Doreen Dodgen-Magee, psychologist and author of *Deviced: Balancing Life and Technology in a Digital World*, internationally known author and speaker, Everytown Survivor Fellow and National Trainer

Rev. Sharon Risher
WITH SHERRI WOOD EMMONS

For Such a Time as This

HOPE AND FORGIVENESS AFTER
THE CHARLESTON MASSACRE

FOREWORD BY REV. DR. MICHAEL W. WATERS

chalice
press
Saint Louis, Missouri

An imprint of Christian Board of Publication

Cover design: Paul Soupiset

Cover art: AdobeStock

ChalicePress.com

Print: 9780827243231
EPUB: 9780827243248
EPDF: 9780827243255

Contents

Acknowledgments

I always felt that I had a book in me. I thought I would write about my life growing up in Charleston and how its Geechie culture influenced the best of and worst of my life. The death of my mother, Mrs. Ethel Lance, and the eight others, as well as the survivors, in Emanuel AME Church, Charleston, South Carolina, has changed the total story, but added so much more.

First, I have to give honor and glory to God.

Momma: My whole life I wanted to make you proud of me. I wanted you to know giving birth to me was the right thing to do. You spent your life striving for more, wanting to learn more, working hard for your family, along with Daddy, Nathaniel Nathan Lance, and showed me how your faith can get you through anything. Your life will serve as a beacon of hope and courage and resiliency. Now people from all over this world have read or heard your name and seen your face. Your death will not be in vain. I promised myself since June 15, 2015, I will spend the rest of my life advocating for change. This book is to honor you.

Brandon and Aja, my dear children: You two are the best of me and your dad. My prayer has always been, thank you, God, for taking care of my children when I didn't. You watched me fail, go through depression, drug addiction, divorce, and still you two made a way for yourselves. I don't know how I would have survived without you two after Momma was killed. You held me up and cheered me on. You have allowed me to love you in my own way. I'm so very proud of the caring, smart, compassionate people you are. Being your mother has been the hardest job and best job of my life. My love for you made me want to do better. I wish you both a life filled with love and peace.

Bernard: In the midst of everything we went through as a couple, you have always been one of my biggest supporters. Your insights and wisdom have always been there for me. Thank you for being a part of my life and for being the Dad you are to our children!

To my sisters, Terrie and Esther, who have gone on to glory, our lives were so intertwined, my life has an emptiness only you two can fill. Esther, I miss your laughter, your humor, and big heart, "Hold my hand Pastor."

To Nadine and Gary, the bloodline, the memories we share, will always be. Blood is thicker than water. To Jonquil Lance Sr., and Jonquil Jr., Auntie will always be there for you!

Austin Presbyterian Theological Seminary: The years I spent in seminary were a time of healing and learning. I was given the opportunity to grow and be happy with my authentic self. I was able to find the best Sharon. The relationships and friendships that were made are still precious to this day. I want to acknowledge Rev. James Lee, who recruited me and became my mentor. He ministered with love and compassion and was always willing to guide you to becoming your best self.

Mike Waters: Mike is the most pastoral person I know. Thank you for all you have contributed in making this book real. Mike's brilliance in preaching, writing, and taking care of people through his social justice activism is beyond measure. I'm grateful for the relationship we have as friends and colleagues. Thank you for all you do for the kingdom.

Abigail Pesta: Abby, without you, this book wouldn't be happening. You were the first person to believe this book could happen. You have been with me every step of the way, and I'm forever thankful for our friendship. Writing the words through other people's voices is truly your God-given gift. No one does it like you. Much love.

Lucy McBath: Our lives were shattered, but you helped me navigate through such pain and grief. Your friendship and mentorship helped me to find my voice and then to use it to invoke change. I will always cherish our friendship and sisterhood.

Sherri Woods Emmons: Thank you for using your gifts to make this book come to life. You were able to capture the essence of who I am. I'm grateful!

Chalice Press: I want to thank the publishing team, especially Brad Lyons, Deborah Arca, Gail Stobaugh, and Connie Wang for their belief in making this book happen. I'm most humbled and grateful for their guidance and willingness to take a chance on me.

Lynn Johnston, Literary Agent: I can't thank you enough for your guidance in navigating my way through the book publishing world. Your expertise is unmatchable.

Foreword

*"We have come over a way that with tears
has been watered. We have come treading our path through the
blood of the slaughtered."* – James Weldon Johnson, 1899

"We gon' be alright." – Kendrick Lamar, 2016

Certain tragedies are forever etched into your memory.

It was a Wednesday in June. I was in Portland, Oregon, a finalist for a national fellowship. After two intensive days of workshops and presentations, I returned to my hotel room exhausted and collapsed on the bed. I made the ill-considered decision to watch some television, but my eyelids soon came clearest in view.

As I briefly woke from my hasty slumber, I noticed a news thread running at the bottom of the screen. There had been a shooting at a church. I remember thinking, "That's terrible," but I soon turned over and drifted back to sleep. Ashamedly, I did not give the news proper attention. The frequency of shootings in our nation tempered my initial response. When I stirred an hour later, the magnitude of the tragedy struck me. No longer was it just a thread at the bottom of the screen. There was a church and emergency lights. There was also a name: Mother Emanuel A.M.E. Church. Hauntingly, there was also a victim count.

Nine persons were dead.

I was glued to the news as more details concerning the massacre were reported. The bullets were unleashed at a Bible study. The murderer was a young white male with a penchant for posing with guns and Confederate flags. All the victims were Black. The first victim was the church's pastor and a state senator. The majority of the victims were women. The pastor's wife and one of their daughters hid in the pastor's study as the massacre unfolded. The murderer's stated purpose was to protect white women from being raped by Black men. He wanted to start a race war.

Certain persons enter your life that help shape and direct your life's path forward. For me, the Reverend Sharon Risher is one such person. Sharon was a chaplain at Parkland Hospital in Dallas, the same hospital where one of America's most famous shooting victims, President John

F. Kennedy, was taken in 1963, the same hospital where the majority of police officers shot in downtown Dallas in 2016 following a nonviolent protest and march for two other shooting victims—Alton Sterling in Baton Rouge, and Philando Castile in Falcon Heights, Minnesota—had also been taken.

It is painful to note that we can mark time in America by who has been shot and when.

The Reverend Freedom McAdoo, a seminarian and chaplain intern who was also a ministerial candidate of our church, contacted me to share that one of her colleagues had lost her mother during the terrorist attack in Charleston. She believed that our church could support Sharon in the midst of such tragedy. I readily agreed. As an A.M.E. church pastor, I also felt it appropriate that all the compassion and concern that had been directed toward our church should be redirected toward an actual family member of a victim.

I remember the first Sunday Sharon literally rolled into our sanctuary. Her foot was still healing from a recent procedure, and she was using a knee scooter to get around. I felt it would be appropriate to acknowledge her presence, but I did not want to overwhelm her by obligating her to speak. In fact, I did not know if she would be able to speak at all. In retrospect it is clear that I did not know Sharon at all. In her clear and angelically raspy voice, Sharon stood courageously and spoke with an unguarded transparency that is a hallmark of her character and personality. She spoke of the heartache and pain that she was experiencing, and she openly acknowledged that she was not yet ready to forgive the terrorist who took her mother's life. However, with time, and the help of God, she was open to that possibility. I marveled at how someone who had experienced such a tragedy and such great loss could even form her mouth to speak or had such strength to stand.

This was my introduction to the force of nature that is Sharon Risher.

No one signs up for tragedy. No one signs up to become a mouthpiece for a movement. No one signs up to daily carry such a heavy mantle of justice. No one signs up to have their most intimate emotions on display for the world. Yet Sharon Risher has done this all with strength and grace that itself gives testimony to the abiding presence of an omnipotent God.

As Sharon continues to stand and speak all across the nation, the stakes get higher and the platforms greater. In short order she has become one of the most prominent voices against racial violence and gun violence in America, and she has become one of the leading advocates for national gun reform. Whether testifying before Congress, appearing on national television, speaking at a rally or on a college campus, at the White House, or in casual conversation, Sharon's heart and compassion for the betterment of our society shines through.

For such a time as this, our nation desperately needs Sharon's voice and her courage. And our nation desperately needs this book. It is stunning, heartbreaking, uplifting, and ultimately, transforming.

The massacre at Mother Emanuel A.M.E. Church remains one of the greatest tragedies of our time. It was a watershed moment in our nation's violent and tumultuous history. In the wake of Charleston, we have had to return to the bitter well of gun violence many, many times. San Bernardino. Orlando. Las Vegas. Sutherland Springs. Parkland. Tree of Life. Too many. We can still mark time by who has been shot and when. Oft times it appears as if we are just buying time until the next mass shooting.

One December I sat in the waiting room of another Dallas hospital while my mother was having a procedure. My phone rang. Any other time I would have rejected the call. But it was Sharon. And I knew that the trial for her mother's killer had begun. I also knew that she needed me to be present and listen.

As she spoke, through tears, Sharon shared how hard it was to be present in that space. She openly shared that she was still on a journey to forgive the killer, but she had not arrived there yet. Sharon was still open to that possibility. Then somehow, again, as testimony to the power of God at work in her, she uttered words from the chorus of a shared favored song. "We gon' be alright!"

Our nation owes a debt of gratitude to Sharon Risher for hewing out of darkness such light. And assuredly, with the power of God, and the prophetic witness of Sharon Risher, one day, we will be alright.

Michael W. Waters

Prologue

On the evening of June 17, 2015, Dylann Roof walked into historic Emanuel African Methodist Church in downtown Charleston, South Carolina, and joined a group of parishioners gathered for their regular Wednesday Bible study. Emanuel AME is one of the oldest African American churches in the South and has a long history of social justice engagement.

The black congregants warmly welcomed the young white stranger into their group, unaware that he was an avowed white supremacist. They were solidly engaged in learning as Roof stayed nearly an hour with them, quietly listening as they reviewed various passages of Scripture from their study sheet. They had given Roof a copy so he could join in. When the group rose and bowed their heads for a closing prayer, Roof reached into his backpack, pulled out a .45-caliber Glock 41 handgun and began shooting. By the time his rampage ended, he had slaughtered nine people.

As Roof carried out his murderous mission, the Reverend Sharon Risher, a hospital chaplain working in Dallas, was busily engaged in her duties, helping the hurting and distraught. Little did she know she was about to become one of them. Among the lives taken at Mother Emanuel that evening were those of Sharon's mother, two cousins, and a dear childhood friend. The Charleston church shootings thrust Rev. Risher into the national spotlight. She has since become a passionate activist for sensible gun laws in the United States.

This is her story.

Sherri Wood Emmons

CHAPTER 1

June 17, 2015

"Granddaddy done had a good life. We knew this was gonna happen."

It was a regular Wednesday night at the Dallas hospital where I worked as a chaplain. I was helping a family whose patriarch had died. They were unusually stoic, so I offered to pray with them.

As I prepared to complete the customary paperwork with the family, I realized I didn't have it with me. I excused myself and went to my office. I still think my forgetting those papers was an intervention by the spirit of God.

I had left my phone charging on my desk and decided to take a moment to check my messages. I'd missed several calls from my daughter, Aja.

The reception was bad in my office, so I took my phone into a conference room and wiggled my way into the corner where I knew I could get a strong signal.

"Aja?"

"Mama, JonQuil called me. Something's going on at the church in Charleston. Granny's church."

My mother's church was Emanuel African American Methodist Episcopal Church. We all called it Mother Emanuel.

Aja told me all the information she'd been able to gather. My sister's son, JonQuil, told her something bad had happened at the church, but he had been unable to get more details. He and his mother, Esther, were going down to the church to see what they could find out.

I had a really bad feeling, but I brushed it aside because had to do my job. A family was processing the death of their grandfather.

You don't know what's happening yet in Charleston. Go and help these people who lost their granddaddy, then get back to your office so you can start calling people.

As soon as I returned to my office, I started making calls. I got through to my baby sister, Nadine, who lives in Charleston. She hadn't heard anything, but she was going to go check it out: "I'm putting on some clothes and going down there to the church."

I called JonQuil. He told me, "Auntie, we down at the church but nobody's letting us get close to the building." His tone conveyed his concern. "They just keep saying something happened in the church. Maybe some shooting. We don't know."

He said authorities were gathering family members at a nearby hotel. So while everybody was there, holding onto each other, I was in Dallas alone. I kept calling my nephew and my sisters, but the calls went to voicemail.

Whatever was going on, I knew Momma would have been at church that evening. Every Wednesday there was a Bible study, and she made it her business to be there and make sure the church was ready. She opened the doors and was always one of the last people to leave that church—every night. My mother *loved* that church. As long as she was able to get out of her bed, Ethel Lance was gonna be at that church—you could count on it.

One time she said to me, "For all the things that I might not have done right in my life, the more time I spend in this church, the more I get to talk to God and ask for forgiveness."

"Ma, I don't think you did so many things wrong."

Her tone turned maternal. "Hey, you never stop asking God for strength and forgiveness."

Every Sunday, she loved to discuss the sermon with me after church. She would call and say, "Girl, Rev. Pinckney throwed *down* today."

I knew she was gone. I had nothing to confirm it, but I just knew. My shift wasn't over for another hour, but I needed to get home. I left early. I had to pull off the road twice because I was crying so hard. The usual twenty-five–minute drive took me an hour that night.

By the time I got home, the nightly news broadcast was filling in some of the details my family couldn't. A gunman had entered Mother Emanuel and started shooting. I kept saying to myself: *This can't be happening. This just can't be happening.* There was no mention of fatalities at that point. The reporters kept repeating that they didn't have all the details.

My head felt like it was exploding. I couldn't think. I didn't want to be by myself. But who could I call to be with me?

I paced my apartment smoking cigarettes, drinking coffee, and staring at the news. I kept reaching out to family members—calling, and calling, and calling. No one answered.

I drifted off to sleep on the couch, likely out of sheer exhaustion.

Finally, my niece, Najee, called about three in the morning. She was with a FBI chaplain. She confirmed what I already knew in my spirit but hoped I would never hear: Momma was in the church.

Momma was dead.

My body felt like it would crumble. I already knew something bad had happened, but I just kept thinking it couldn't really be *that* bad.

I heard screams. They were mine. Screaming was all I could do. I don't remember the rest of the conversation with Najee and the chaplain. My poor dog Puff. He had never heard a guttural sound like that coming from his favorite human, so he started barking. *Oh Lord, I gotta stop screaming. It's three o'clock in the morning and there are people living upstairs. I gotta get myself together.* I *made* myself stop screaming.

When I finally calmed down, I grabbed Puff and fell down onto the couch. Lying in a semi-catatonic state, I held onto Puff and I just cried. I was on my own. *Who can I call at this time of night? Who can I call? I can't call nobody.* I was in that abyss that we sing about so often the in the Black Church—that time when you're poignantly aware that you have nobody but Jesus to talk to.

Later that morning I called my boss at the hospital. It went directly to her voicemail. "Linda, I wanted to let you know that my momma was killed last night in the Charleston church shooting." I guess I was blunt, but I didn't know a better way to say that I was in the midst of the worst tragedy of my life.

Finally, I called my son, Brandon. We talked and we cried. And then we cried some more. We decided not to call Aja right away. I knew she would be exhausted. She had been up all night. *Let her sleep. God knows, we all needed some sleep.*

For the next two days, I stayed in my pajamas. I didn't even bother to shower. I didn't eat. I didn't sleep. I drank coffee and smoked cigarettes.

I didn't leave my apartment. I couldn't pull myself away from the television updates that really didn't tell me anything new. Still, I wanted to see everything. *Maybe it was a mistake. Maybe they'll find out that Momma was in the bathroom when the shooting happened. She could have been cleaning up. That's what she did! Maybe she got the chance to hide somewhere. I know she was in the church, but maybe she found a way to escape the carnage. She can't really be dead.* Everything was a blur.

My support system in Dallas wasn't very big. I had friends at work, but we didn't do a lot together outside of work. I knew people at the church I'd been attending, but ministers generally don't form personal relationships with the people in the church.

Truthfully, even before the tragedy, I had started to pull away from that church because I realized that I was going nowhere in ministry there. So maybe the people at the church really didn't know how to deal with me in the aftermath.

Despite the distant relationship, the morning after the shootings, the pastor and the bishop of the district came to see me. I was looking like hell run over, and I knew it. I didn't care. I was just a mess.

"What can the church do to support you?" They asked with genuine concern.

Well, I needed to get reservations to go home. But where would the extra money come from? Hospital chaplains don't make a lot of money, and I didn't have an emergency fund for something like this.

They already had a check prepared.

Then the bishop asked if I would do a press conference.

My immediate thought was, *This lady must be crazy.* I was sure my thought showed on my face. "Press conference? No, I'm not gonna be able to do a press conference. And please at this time don't divulge my name."

They respected my wishes. When the Texas news airwaves reported there was a Dallas connection to the killings, they just said a chaplain from Parkland Hospital.

At some point during those first days my boss and two of my coworkers came to see me. I don't remember a lot about the visit, but I remember they brought food and an envelope of money they had collected.

I spent a lot of time on the phone those first two days, talking with Brandon and Aja, and my sister Esther. She was having a very hard time. Her son JonQuil thought he might have to take her to the emergency room at one point. She couldn't stop crying.

Esther, hold on. Hold on, Esther. I'm coming. I was the oldest, and Esther always gave me the respect of an elder. I kept trying to reassure her on the phone, "Hold on, Esther. I'm coming. I'm coming."

My kids then were just as dazed as I was; still, they were trying to make sure that their mother was okay. For them, it was like walking on eggshells. They didn't know what to say; and if they did, would it set me off on another crying binge?

I'm kind of like my momma when it comes to giving attention to details. I'm a planner, so I was trying to make sure things were being arranged while I collected myself to make the plane trip home. "Okay, what time am I gonna leave? You know I want to get to Charleston early. Let's not mess around." So I was probably getting on their nerves. But they were focused on making sure that I was able to get to Charleston.

Even after days of watching, I could not tear myself away from the television. If I was awake, the TV was on. The day after the murders, the police arrested Dylann Roof—I hate to even acknowledge his name. The news outlets had been showing a video of him leaving the church. The next day a woman recognized him driving his car and called the police. He was taken to jail in North Charleston.

Evil.

The first time I saw him, saw his face, he personified evil to me. I was stunned by his youth, though. *How did such a young boy get so much hate inside him?* His eyes looked dead. That picture they showed of him with that little smirk on his face—I hate to see that picture because it represents pure evil to me. It's gotten better for me as time has passed, but that look in his eyes is just haunting.

I was captivated by the proceedings on television. *Praise God! You are not gonna get away with this. They got you now. They got you now.*

On June 19, Dylann Roof appeared in court by video from the jail. The whole thing was televised, and I was transfixed on the screen, still watching from Dallas.

How could this be? How could this be? They are actually talking about my momma, a little old lady who—I mean, not an old lady, because Momma was so spry and spunky—but a person who, you know, wasn't nobody. She was everything to her family, but she was kind of nobody in the grand scheme of things—just a nameless black woman who faithfully went to church every chance she got—except to us. And now her name was on nationwide TV. She was killed in church by this little fool. I just could not understand.

Many of the victims' relatives attended the hearing, and I was feeling guilty because I wasn't there. I felt like I should have been there with my sisters, Nadine and Esther. Since Momma had died, that sort of made me the family matriarch.

The judge extended an unexpected invitation to family members to address the killer. I later learned that since none of the family members had prepared statements, no one was planning to say anything.

Nadine accepted the judge's offer. As she walked toward the podium, everybody looked at each other like, *Oh hell. We don't know what is getting ready to come out of her mouth*—because, honestly, we just never did know what our sister would say.

True to her reputation, she said something totally unexpected, just what would be expected from her. "I forgive you. You took something very precious away from me. I will never get to talk to her ever again—but I forgive you, and have mercy on your soul... You hurt me. You hurt a lot of people. If God forgives you, I forgive you."

I started screaming again. Nadine's words went through me hard, like an electric shock. I wasn't ready to forgive. *Did she think she was speaking for the entire family? How dare she?!*

I felt faint. I was light-headed and my stomach felt like it had dropped—upside down. I stayed on the couch holding my precious Puff while the tears rolled down my cheeks. The daughter's raw hurt forced its way in front of the measured composure of the ordained minister who dealt with grief and hurt on a daily basis. I have studied the Bible for scholarly and for personal reasons. I know that God commands us to forgive, but I was not ready to forgive this monster who killed my mother.

People can judge me any way they want. Forgiveness is a process. I will get there when I get there. I answer to God.

My faith had carried me through many life hurdles. But could it carry me over this mountain of grief, anger, and loss?

CHAPTER 2

Life with Momma

Ethel and Nathaniel Lance reared five children—Sharon, Terrie, Gary, Esther, and Nadine. All of us kids got along, mainly because we didn't have a choice. The other reason why was because there was lots of love in our home—though never enough space in that tiny house! We lived in a two-bedroom place back then, and we were always on top of each other.

Our tiny home was situated in a black neighborhood on the east side of Charleston. The streets had historic names, like Washington and Calhoun. It was a pretty run-down area and everything just looked beat up. Parents worked hard. Kids went to school and played in the yard or in the park—kickball, softball, jump rope.

We lived really close to Calhoun Street Park, which was run by Charleston's Parks and Recreation Department for black kids on that side of town. The park was a hub within the community, where they offered organized basketball, softball, and arts and crafts. If you had sense enough to take advantage of stuff, they had everything going on at the park.

That's where I met Myra Singleton (Thompson, after her marriage), who was killed with Momma at Emanuel. Myra grew up in the same neighborhood as me. She ended up getting attached to the Coakley family because there were some circumstances in her own family that weren't good. The Coakleys took her in.

There were a lot of Coakleys! The matriarch, Miss Sarah, was a beautiful Cherokee-looking lady. She was a staunch member of Emanuel Church. Mr. Coakley was very, very quiet.

It seemed like everybody went through that house because the Coakleys lived near Calhoun Street Park, where we all played. Plus, the Coakleys were very athletic. They played basketball, they played softball.

Myra and I became fast friends. Even after my family moved to public housing, we still went to high school together.

Myra was just a nice girl. In the summer, we would play "school" in the Coakleys' front yard. Myra and twins Claudette and Catherine Coakley were older girls, so they got to be the teachers. We would each pay our little five cents or whatever, and they would have pencils and paper, and they would teach us math and all of this. And then we'd have our little lunch break where we might get a sandwich or something. Myra and all of them ended up being educators.

My parents lived paycheck to paycheck, but I never really knew that as a kid. I never felt hungry or cold or poor. I just remember that we never seemed to have enough space. We had one bedroom for all the kids back then. The girls had to double up in bunk beds and our brother had a bed to himself. I shared my bed with Esther, and for a while Terrie had her own bed. Then, when Nadine was born, she slept in the bed with Terrie. That's just how things were in those days, and I didn't really mind, except that Esther was always peeing the damned bed! Later, we found out that she had a kidney problem, but all I knew back then was that I would wake up every morning with a peed-up damned bed.

Terrie and I were two years apart. We were close, but we fought a lot because she would wear my clothes without my permission. I'd save my little money and buy particular little pieces of clothing, and she would just wear them!

Esther was always a bit overweight and that bothered her a lot, but she always had a smile. Momma used to talk about how hard it was to find youthful clothes in Esther's size. Esther was the funny, jovial sibling who always wanted to have fun. She has always been willing to help people out, even at her own expense. If someone asks her for money, she will give it to them, even if it means she can't pay her own bills. That's just Esther.

As a child, she loved to dance and sing. I remember us girls dancing and singing to all those women's groups that were popular in the 'Sixties and early 'Seventies—the Supremes, the Shirelles, the Ronettes. Pick a group and we were singing their hit songs. Of course, being the oldest, I was always the lead singer—especially Diana Ross! The front porch was our stage, and hairbrushes were our microphones.

Our brother, Gary, was always messing something up, but he got away with it because he was the only boy. My parents learned very early on that Gary was nearly deaf, and that was a struggle. Kids would call him names like "Deaf and Dumb" or call him "retarded." I would be very protective of him, being the oldest. Sometimes I would push people and say, "Don't talk about my brother like that!"

We coddled him, though, because of his disability—especially Momma; but, Daddy not so much.

Momma somehow found the means to send Gary to Memminger Elementary School, one of the only schools in Charleston that had a program for deaf children. Momma really had to fight to get Gary into that school because it wasn't in our district. To this day, I don't know how she paid for that, but she did.

If any of her kids needed something, Momma made sure we had it.

After elementary school, Gary went to the South Carolina School for the Deaf and Blind in Spartanburg. He spent a couple of years there but dropped out by the time he got to the tenth grade.

Momma took a class and learned basic signing so she could communicate better with Gary. Nobody else in the family could sign. Years later, my son asked me, "Why didn't everybody to learn to sign?"

I responded, "You know what, Brandon? That's a good question," though I really didn't have answer to give him. I guess we already had learned to communicate with Gary in our own ways. He had some hearing, so once he got his hearing aid, he would get what you were talking about. Or maybe that's the justification I give myself. We were just kids, and it was something we didn't even think about.

And Gary can speak, to some degree. If you have been around him enough, he can talk to you and you can figure what he's saying. So we just went with that, and Gary learned how to get by.

One Christmas, when I was twelve or thirteen, every one of us kids got bikes. I rode mine for a while, and then I kind of put it down. Gary messed his up, so he started taking parts off of mine. So then there I was with no bike while he was out riding with my bicycle parts! That was Gary.

Nadine is the baby of the family, so, from her birth, everything was all about her! She was our baby. Plus, she never experienced the harder times we had earlier while we were growing up. By the time she was born, Momma had a job working for the city, and Daddy had started working on the waterfront, and our little family was kind of groovin' nicely.

Nadine was always meticulous about her clothes and her hair. One year, Nadine was crowned Little Miss Something at Sanders-Clyde Elementary School. We all were so proud of her. I came all the way from college in Charlotte, North Carolina, for that thing. Everyone in the family was there for Nadine, Miss Little Thing, Miss Princess, because that's what she was!

I had to take care of Nadine when she was little, so I took her with me everywhere. When I played softball, I had to take Nadine to all the games, and everybody made a fuss over her.

Because I was the oldest, Momma depended on me to kind of shepherd all the younger kids. But Nadine needed more care than the rest of them. When Momma and Daddy would go out and I would be left in charge, our house would be like a damned menagerie—*a zoo!* There always would be a mutiny, because they would all be against me. I'd be saying, "Ya'll can't do that!" And they'd just laugh.

Our parents worked all the time, it seemed, but on the few occasions when Momma and Daddy were home, and they'd sit around after dinner or watch TV, the kids would get into wrestling tag teams. Momma and Daddy would sit on the couch and watch us wrestling around and just laugh. If we got too aggressive, they would intervene: "All right, all right, that's enough now." It would always be me and Esther against Terrie and Gary. Nadine was too little to be involved in any of that.

When I was little, Momma worked for several white families, doing ironing and cleaning. That was some hard work. But when I was nine or ten, she got a job in maintenance at the new Gaillard Center, a concert hall and performance venue that had just been built. Daddy was a brick mason, and later he worked as a longshoreman on the Charleston docks.

Momma wanted a better life for her kids. She didn't have much schooling herself, but she wanted her children to be educated. She would always find free things for us to do, often educational events. She'd take us to programs in the park, at a local museum, or at the zoo in nearby Hampton Park.

I walked to school in the mornings with my siblings, after Momma helped us get ready. Buist Elementary was right across the street from Mother Emanuel AME Church. Our route was peppered with people who knew our parents, especially our daddy, Nathaniel. He was quite popular in the neighborhood. His nickname was "Lima Bean." He loved lima beans and could cook the hell out of them. Nobody else cooked them like Daddy. Along our walk to school, we gathered up other kids, arriving at school in a group.

Momma encouraged each of her children to pursue higher education, because she hadn't finished high school. Then, because she felt so strongly about education, she enrolled at Charles A. Brown Adult Night School in Charleston and received her high school diploma the same year that I graduated from that same school. That was a memorable moment for my family. We were the first people in our family to finish high school. I continued my education and became the first family member to graduate from college. A year later, Terrie received her degree. Our family was accomplishing things Momma had dreamed could happen; things she worked hard to make possible.

We had a praying Momma who had a big heart and was always willing to help somebody else. Momma would always say, "Every man for himself, and God for us all."

She loved wearing fine perfumes and dancing to James Brown's music. Momma was a no-nonsense kind of woman had a very strict work ethic. She kept her home clean and spotless.

On special occasions, when we got dressed up in our Sunday clothes, Momma would spray us with one of her perfumes. Then she would hide the bottle, because she knew, given the chance, we'd be spraying it all over the place. Oh, she loved her perfumes! One time when I was a little bit older, I bought her a fragrance at Edward's Five and Dime store. It was "eau de something." I was really proud of buying that bottle of perfume with my own money, which I had earned from running errands for the neighborhood ladies.

When I gave it to Momma, she said, "What a nice gift!" She acted like it was the best fragrance in the world.

When we were *really* young, my parents didn't go to church, but they did encourage us to pray. For Momma, Sunday was a day to relax. I mean, with five kids and a fulltime job, and trying to figure it all out, she needed that day off. But that was one thing about my Momma, if you wanted to do something that she felt was good for you, she was gonna make *sure* that you could participate to the fullest.

My girlfriend Jewel, who lived across the street, asked me if I wanted to go to church one day, and her grandmother took us. I started going regularly. Going to church is what you did on a Sunday if you were a kid in a black neighborhood. Momma was all on board with me going. She even tried to push my sisters and brother to go sometimes, but church was kind of my own little world that I carved out for myself.

Momma helped me get dressed every Sunday that I went with Jewel to the Macedonia African Methodist Episcopal Church. It was a small congregation of regular working people. I felt right at home there. I didn't know much about God then. All I knew was that church was the place where people said God was. I knew this God person was special and I wanted to please him.

That church became a place where I felt peaceful and safe. I remember opening the door and stepping inside, and just feeling the warmth. Sometimes I would show up early and listen to the adults rehearsing the songs in the back. I loved the sound of those voices. There was always a lot of vigorous singing. I realized that if I played it smart, one day I might get to sing in the choir, or read scripture in front of everyone. I really wanted to read a scripture passage.

As a kid, I always wanted to be in the spotlight. I credit Momma for that. She had a quiet way of making me feel like I could do anything. I knew she was always beside me, lending her support. She didn't broadcast it. That wasn't who she was. She was not a warm and fuzzy kind of person. She was formidable, but I always knew I had her support.

On Easter, the kids would stand up in the church and give little speeches. I really looked forward to giving my own speech. I went to church all dressed up with my hair done. Usually I wore ponytails, but that Sunday Momma took a warm comb and straightened my hair. I had long, silky hair, and, on Easter, I got to wear my hair down. I can still remember my first Easter speech. I had learned those words well. You had to memorize the thing—no reading from paper. I was proud of myself for writing and memorizing two whole lines instead of just a few words. I was ready; I wanted to say it like a pro. I stood up and confidently recited my speech, which was more like a poem:

"The daffodils are blowing.
They raise their heads of gold.
They seem to tell a story that often times is told.
Happy Easter!"

Momma came to church that Sunday, and I knew she was proud of me.

One day in 1967, when I was nine years old, Momma called the house and told me to put on my Sunday clothes and come down to the County Hall. She wanted me to see somebody very important.

One of Momma's managers at the Gaillard Center helped manage events at the County Hall, a black entertainment venue. It was one of the few places black people in Charleston could go in those days.

I had never been to County Hall before. Most of the time, the attraction was dancers or other entertainers. When I was in high school, James Brown came to County Hall. It was ninety-nine cents to get in. All my high school buddies were talking about going, but my Momma said, "You are not!" See, County Hall was also notorious for fights. You get a bunch of black people together, and something's getting ready to go down. That's just life, you know? And in her mind, Momma tried to protect me as much as she could from the streets. I didn't go that time, but some other times, I skipped out and did some things I had no right doing. But at that particular time, I was not gonna cross her.

But on that day in 1967, I did what Momma told me to do. I walked through the neighborhood to get to County Hall. In those days, a young girl could walk the neighborhood streets and not worry. None of my siblings came with me, but Momma was waiting at the front door when I got there. That's when she told me that Rev. Dr. Martin Luther King Jr. was speaking that day and she wanted me to hear him. Momma took my hand and led me into the back area of that hall. She was working the event, so she couldn't sit down with me. She settled me at a table in the back. And they served food! It was a plate of roast beef with gravy, mashed potatoes, and green beans. I remember that because I don't think I had ever had roast beef before. That wasn't something we were eating at home.

I was nervous, but I knew that Martin Luther King Jr. was a very great man, and that black people in America loved him. And my momma, knowing that too, wanted me to be a part of that. Something in her said, "I want my child to come and hear this."

It was noisy, but I can remember the electricity in the air—the hum that goes on when you're in a crowded hall and there's expectation and anticipation of what coming. It was just electric!

I couldn't see what was going on, but I could hear Dr. King's voice. He sounded like God to me. He was truly like the messiah of black people. He was like Jesus walking on earth. That's how black people felt about him. This man was speaking truth from a religious point of view, when everything back then was just going crazy. A black person could be killed for talking like that!

He talked about some of the people he knew in Charleston—Herbert Fielding, whose family owned the funeral home, and Judge Daniel Martin, who was a member of Emanuel Church. Those were prominent people in Charleston when I was young. And I was sitting there with them because Momma made sure that happened.

In my young mind, I knew then and there that I wanted to be able to speak like Dr. King. I knew that someday I would stand in front of a crowd, and they would want to hear what I had to say. My life changed that day. Momma made that happen.

I always knew she would break her neck to help me do or have anything I wanted. We didn't have a lot, but our lives were blessed with love for one another.

* * * * *

I think I must have been around six years old when I learned that I had a different father than my sisters and brother. It happened one day when we were visiting my grandma—my daddy's (Nathaniel, aka "Lima Bean") mom. She lived on John's Island, one of the islands around Charleston. All of us kids were playing in the yard, and she was sitting on the porch with a friend. I heard the friend say, "Who dat little red girl?"

She meant me. I was lighter skinned than my siblings.

Then my grandma replied, "That's my son's stepdaughter. That's Lima's child. Well, that ain't Lima's child, but he's raising her."

That's the first time I had ever heard anything like that. I didn't say anything about it to anyone, but the moment stuck with me. It was the first time I really looked at myself and realized that I was different. My mom never made me feel different than anyone else.

After I learned that information, I sometimes wondered about my birth father. *Who was he, really?* I had heard a vague story from my maternal grandmother at some point. When Momma was fourteen, she had fallen for a young Puerto Rican man who wanted to marry her and move her to New York, where he was going with his family. Momma's mother thought she was too young, and so the couple split up. I believed this man was my biological father. I tried a couple times to bring it up with my mom, but it was clear that she did not want to go there. I couldn't figure out why she wouldn't talk about it. I just figured she had been so young when she got pregnant, it was too sticky for her to discuss. But still, I wondered. Something seemed off.

And I was right. I just didn't know it yet.

CHAPTER 3

Momma Gets Jesus

In 1974, my mom got Jesus and started going to Emanuel African Methodist Episcopal Church with my Grandmother Emily. That's what we used call becoming a Christian: "She got Jesus."

Susie Jackson, who died with Momma on that awful night, was a distant cousin to Daddy, so she asked Momma to come to church with her.

Momma fell in *love* with that church. She felt proud of being a part of that congregation. Many of the members there were prominent Charlestonians, like Judge Daniel Martin. A lot of doctors and teachers and lawyers belonged to Emanuel. Momma was just proud to be there with them all. In her mind, I think, my momma always felt inferior. She never really gave herself credit for what she had been through and what she had accomplished. So being there in that church just made her so happy.

I was a teenager by this time, and I started going with her to Emanuel. That church was so much bigger and more formal than the little church I had been attending, but it was still church.

Emanuel is the oldest African Methodist Episcopal Church in the South—founded in 1818. Back then, there were laws in Charleston that allowed black people to worship only during the daytime, and they weren't supposed to be able to read. Police raided the church a few times during its early days, arresting people who were worshiping, fining them, and sometimes sentencing them to whippings.

In 1822, Denmark Vesey, one of the church founders, was accused of plotting a slave revolt. He and several other members were executed, and the church was burned to the ground by a mob. After that, the congregation had to meet in secret for a long time. They finally rebuilt the church after the Civil War.

By the time Momma and I started attending, Emanuel was *the* church for black people in Charleston. The building is a huge, stately edifice. Back then, when you walked into the vestibule there was a table with all the bulletins. The uniformed ushers were at their posts, wearing white gloves. They would open the huge wooden swinging doors that led you into the sanctuary at the appropriate interval.

Even today, when the doors open to the massive sanctuary, you just know you are entering someplace special. Once inside, you step onto the deep, red carpeting that runs down each aisle, separating the rows upon rows of beautiful warm brown wooden pews upholstered with red cushions. Stained-glass windows evenly line both sides of the sanctuary, which has a seating capacity of 2500. The floor-to-ceiling collage of stained-glass windows that serve as a backdrop to the pulpit area are breathtakingly beautiful.

The pulpit area was sacred ground. You did not want to mess around and be walking through the pulpit area if you were a kid, or even an adult. As kids we would sometimes run around inside the church, but we knew better than to go *up there*. Every now and then a young kid might wander up there, and those ladies—the stewards—would about have a stroke!

There's a long aisle from the back of the sanctuary to the pulpit. Holding up the balcony and its massive pipe organ are large wood pillars. From the balcony come the melodious sounds of the hymnal choir, attended by the organ. The gospel choir is seated in the sanctuary in a designated space. Both choirs sing during most of the services.

Sitting inside that church, I knew it was a place of worship. Even though it was very ordered, I knew that I was a part of something special. And to be there when the sun came streaking through the stained-glass windows was a beautiful sight to behold.

At Emanuel, worshipers dressed to impress. I would wear a fancy church dress with stockings every Sunday. Our church clothes and our school clothes did not intermingle. My mom was a stickler about our appearance. She always wanted her children to be well groomed.

All of us teens sat in the back of the church. We'd pass notes and whisper, all under the watchful side-eye of the attending ushers. I knew my momma would not want to get a report that her child was disruptive in church! And even after I was starting to be a little radical, it was still important to me that my mom not be embarrassed.

The church would serve breakfast in the fellowship hall after Sunday school and before the late service. It was a fundraiser. (You know, the church is always having to raise money.) So you could come to Sunday school and afterward there was enough time to grab something to eat before you went into worship. Of course, Momma was on that little kitchen brigade, helping to cook and serve and clean.

The fellowship hall is downstairs from the sanctuary. You go down a narrow way, past the cornerstone of the original church and a hallway that commemorates Emanuel's founders. The hall is a large, spacious room. They have partitioned the sides for Sunday school classrooms. Also down there are the only restrooms in the church, along with the pastor's office and the administrative office.

Back then, we would sit as a family and have breakfast. The menu might include fried fish and grits, or salmon croquettes, or sausage and eggs. You would get a plate of breakfast for about two dollars. It was a time to hang out with your family and see your friends. Momma was working the meal, so she couldn't sit down with us. But she would come over faithfully to make sure we had everything we needed. "You got what you need?" she'd ask.

I remember how proud Momma felt when she became a member of the usher board. Ushers are an important part of the Black Church. They are the gatekeepers and the greeters. They're the first people you see when you walk into the church. They help you find a seat, they collect the offering money, and they generally keep things in order. At Emanuel, they wear a uniform—white or black, depending on the occasion—and white gloves…the whole deal. It's all very organized, and all about protocol. Momma was so proud to put on that uniform! She was an usher there for decades. Then, when she retired from Gaillard Center, she worked as a sexton at Emanuel to help raise money for my niece Najee's education after her mom (Terrie) got sick.

Sometimes I wonder if Momma joined the church to help her escape her troubles at home. Daddy had become a functioning alcoholic. Momma never drank. Sometimes they would fight, and he would get physical with her, or throw dishes. Since I was the oldest, I would have to pick up the pieces of broken dishes. The next morning, my parents would get up and act like nothing had happened. When I got old enough, I would help her fight him. If things got really bad, she would pack us up and we would spend a couple days at Grandmomma's house. But we always would go back home.

It was hard to watch my mom go through that, and I often wondered why she stayed with him. She never wanted to talk about the bad things, though. She always said, "It's okay. It's okay."

Momma put a lot of responsibility on me. I kept her secrets. Sometimes she'd go out with a girlfriend and tell me not to tell Daddy where she was. My dad was very jealous. He knew that I knew her whereabouts. He would try to get me to tell, but I never would. He never got physical with me, but he would talk rough, trying to get it out of me.

Daddy didn't go to church. He would always say, "I don't know why you're going to that damn church. They ain't tellin' you nothing you need to know, no way." He believed he didn't have to go to church to know that he believed in Jesus. That was his thing.

He would say, "There ain't no need for me to lie. I ain't goin' in that church talking about, 'I'm gonna do this, Lord. I'm gonna do that.' No, I'm gonna just be me, and then I ain't got to worry about lyin' to God."

When he drank, Daddy would talk you to death. He would play Barry White all night. And then, at two o'clock in the morning, he would come and sit on the edge of the bed and hold my hand, and say, "I know you're not my seed. I know that. But it's just like you are. And I love you. I want you to know that, Sharon. Wake up, Sharon! Listen to every word I'm telling you."

"Okay, Daddy. I know you love me. I love you."

I had a love/hate relationship with that little short black man who took care of me with everything he had.

We moved into public housing when I was in the tenth grade. For as long back as I could remember, we had lived on Charleston's east side, renting somebody else's house. Then we moved to a multi-family house close to where the medical university is. From there, we ended up moving to a new public housing development that's very close to the cemetery where Momma is now buried. Back then, people would say, "Ohh, I couldn't live next to a cemetery."

Momma would tell them, "You know, it's not the dead you gotta worry about. It's the damn living."

The new place had three bedrooms. Gary shared a room with Terrie and Nadine, and Esther and I shared a room of our own. Momma felt like it was a good move, but she didn't put Daddy on the lease—because, if she had, we wouldn't have qualified to live there. And oh my, Daddy hated not being on the lease! But it helped our family.

I was very proud of the fact that, even as dysfunctional as we were, we had a Momma and a Daddy—two parents who were working their butts off to do the best they could for us.

At school, all of our teachers were black, and they instilled in us the belief that the way to succeed was to learn. I took that to heart. I knew I wanted to go to college, and I knew I would find a way to get there, even though my family couldn't afford it. My teachers saw that thirst in me and pushed me to excel. They told me I could get grants for college. Our teachers were tough, too. Corporal punishment was very much a part of the school system. One teacher would knock your head against the chalkboard if you got a math problem wrong. I was always thinking, *Don't pick me! Especially for long division.*

My junior year in high school, I got involved with student government and I loved it! I ran for vice president on a state level and won. I got to work with kids from schools around South Carolina. I hadn't been around white kids much. When I began meeting them through the student government association, it seemed as if they knew everything there was to know. They were extremely confident. Privately, I was intimidated, but I didn't show it. I spoke up. I just looked at the kids around me and thought, *I'm here too. So y'all got money? That's all right. It's all good.*

They were probably as poor as I was, but as a kid, I thought all white people had money. I watched the way the white kids behaved in social settings. One time, we went to an elegant restaurant, with linen tablecloths and all kinds of utensils. *Damn, I don't know which fork to use.* I didn't want to be the dumb black kid, so I watched which fork the white kids picked up, and did the same.

I took advantage of every opportunity. I joined Upward Bound, the program sponsored by the Department of Education to help low-income kids who had the potential to go to college. The program paid you ten dollars if you showed up to get tutored in math and English at the College of Charleston on a Saturday, so I always went and made my ten bucks. My mom would say, "You know, you gotta give Momma a little bit of that."

On those Saturdays, black kids from the inner city would converge on the college, which had mainly white students. We would sit in a corner of the cafeteria, watching the white kids and giggling. We wondered what they thought of us, but our feeling was, "We're here. Ain't nothing you can do about it."

Upward Bound introduced me to so many things. I went to Cape Canaveral, where I saw a rocket blast off. I was proud because I had helped raise money for the trip. At one point, we all got tickets to see Roberta Flack. Whoa! That was like a real grown-up thing. I got a new outfit for the occasion—white, big-leg bell bottoms, a black-and-white jacket, and platform shoes. I even had a turban made for my head. It was wonderful to hear her sing "Killing Me Softly." What a night!

In 1976, when I was a senior, I got to represent South Carolina at a program in Washington, D.C., where I joined students from across the country to learn about politics and government. I was thrilled! I flew on an airplane by myself for the first time. I stayed in a hotel for a week and met South Carolina senators Strom Thurmond and Fritz Hollings.

My mom was so proud. She bought me a white rabbit fur jacket for the trip. It was fake rabbit, but it was still pretty. I remember her coming home with that jacket. "You're gonna need a good coat," she said. "It's gonna be cold in D.C." I was so proud of that coat.

In Washington, I really thought I was somebody. *Look at this little Geechie girl, here in Washington, D.C.* There was not a lot of balance there when it came to race, but I just chit-chatted with the white kids like I belonged.

I think that's when I started really getting interested in politics. My goal was to graduate from college, then go to law school and become a lawyer, and then enter politics.

CHAPTER 4

College Girl, Addict, Chaplain

In the fall of 1976, I packed my clothes and headed to Johnson C. Smith University in Charlotte. I had a little piece of a scholarship and some federal grants. My parents drove me to the campus in their station wagon. We cried up a bucket as we said our goodbyes.

I had just a few things for my dorm room: a little black-and-white TV, an electric typewriter, and some cassette tapes of my favorite bands—Chicago, Average White Band, and Earth, Wind & Fire. The students there were from all over the country—New York, D.C., Philadelphia. They made fun of my South Carolina accent. I laughed it off, but it bothered me. It reminded me of when I was a kid and had a lisp. I got pulled out of class to work with a speech therapist, and it was embarrassing. So I started paying attention to how I formed my words. *No one will laugh at me because of the way I sound.*

Otherwise, I embraced college. I became a flag girl. I majored in political science because I wanted to be a lawyer.

My sister Terrie was two years younger than me, but she had skipped a grade in high school, so she was just a year behind me in school. And wasn't Momma proud to have two of her daughters going to college?

Terrie did her first year at St. Augustine's University in Raleigh, North Carolina. And then she just popped up at Smith: "Hey. I transferred. Here I am."

And I was looking at her like, *What?* But I was glad to have my sister there with me.

Sometimes Nadine or Esther would come to visit. I remember Esther saying, sometime later, "You know, we were proud of our big sister living in another city, because that gave us someplace to go." Not a lot of the people she knew had a big sister in college, and it was special for my family because I was the first.

While we were away at school, my mom was struggling with some things at home—especially with my brother, Gary.

My brother always seems to have had things not go in his favor. He made a lot of bad decisions that got him in a lot of trouble. Eventually he had to spend time in prison. But guess who would visit him every chance she got? There was never a time when there were visiting hours for Gary that Momma was not there.

Several times when I came home from Charlotte, I visited Gary too. Going through the ID process, having them searching through your bag and everything, and then going through those doors that clanged shut behind you—it's scary! But he would always be glad to see us.

We had a cousin in the same jail as Gary, and his momma would be there, too, so it was like a damned family reunion. But Gary and my cousin appreciated that they had people who would come to visit.

During my senior year of college, I met Howard Bernard Risher. He was the brother of a girl I knew, and we happened to meet at a mall while I was home on a break. Bernard was working on his master's degree in psychology at the Citadel. He asked me for my number, and we went on a date to see *Superman* before I went back to school. We stayed in touch over the months, talking on the phone. He came from a good family, had a solid education, and played the saxophone in a band. *Wow, I'm coming up in the world*, I thought.

Pretty soon, we fell in love and wanted to spend all our time together. I was going to come home from college to spend that summer with Bernard. Momma did not like that. "Oh my God, no! You gonna come home and shack up? And he's a preacher's kid, too. Oh my God! What you think you doing?"

Bernard and I discussed it and decided, "Well, to shut them up we might as well just get married." And that's what we did.

We got married in June of 1979. His daddy conducted the ceremony, which was very casual. I wore a halter top and jeans. It was just us. I didn't even tell my parents we were getting married. After the ceremony, we just kind of popped it on them.

After I graduated from Smith, we had a big wedding reception at the Gaillard Center. We were able to get the hall *free* because Momma worked there. That was a big deal!

In the beginning, Momma didn't like Bernard very much because she felt like he had this air about him. I think that came from her always feeling like people were better than her. Bernard's dad was a well-known minister and his mom was a teacher. They were college educated. That mattered to Momma—how things looked. I think that's why she tried so hard to have nice things and to look good, so people would not judge her. She warmed up to Bernard eventually. And she tried to be happy for me—because she didn't have a choice.

At some point that year, Terrie's roommate situation at Smith wasn't working out, so she ended up living with Bernard and me for a while. And even after she graduated from college, she lived in the same apartment complex we did. My younger sisters visited sometimes, too.

We had plans, but I didn't become a lawyer, and Bernard didn't become a psychologist. We were young, and we thought love was enough to carry us through, so we got a place in Charlotte and found jobs to pay the bills. I worked as a clerk at a Trailways bus station, then later in a one-woman law office, working for Miss Patricia King, where I learned to be a paralegal. Bernard worked for UPS. Within five years, we had two kids, Brandon and Aja. We did all right, at least at first.

Terrie loved to babysit when Brandon was little. She loved her some Brandon! It was good to have my sister close by. When Brandon got christened, everybody came from Charleston. Bernard's family was there, and so was mine.

Tragedy struck my family a few years later—one of many to come. Wednesday was payday for the longshoremen working on the docks. Everybody knew it. My dad picked up his paycheck that day, like he always did. Daddy got robbed. Someone hit him so hard that he fell to the ground and lay there, unconscious. A passerby saw him and called the police, saying there was a drunk man lying in the street. He wasn't drunk; he was paralyzed. He would never move again.

He and my mom were separated at that point, but she offered to take him back home. He chose to live with his mother instead. My sister Terrie, who had been living in Charlotte, decided to move to Charleston to care for him. I begged her not to move back. I knew Charleston would not be fruitful for her. She was smart as a damned whip, had a computer-science degree, and there were very few women in that field back then.

I couldn't understand why she would want to go back to Charleston. Why would you want to go back to a place where there weren't really any jobs in her field? To me, Charleston meant struggle and nothingness. I didn't see a future in Charleston and knew that I had to leave because the opportunities just weren't there for me.

Sadly, my fears for Terrie came true. Daddy was terribly depressed. And something in her just snapped. She began to suffer from mental health issues. Doctors prescribed a drug to treat mood disorders, but she said it made her feel like a zombie. One time when I went to visit, she was off her medication and had a manic episode. She grabbed me 'round my neck until I nearly blacked out. I had red rings around my neck. I got the hell up out of Charleston soon after that!

Terrie continued to spiral downward, self-medicating with drugs. I believe to this day her life might have been very different had she not moved back to Charleston. But eventually, something wonderful happened: Terrie started going to Mother Emanuel again and she managed to get it together.

We always believed that no matter what happened, the church was gonna keep us going. And it did.

My father died about a year after he was attacked. I think he willed himself to die. He would always tell me, "If I can't be who I am, there's no reason to live."

"Daddy, don't talk like that!" I would tell him, but I know he wanted out.

Bernard and I made it through nineteen years together before we fell apart. That was much longer than anyone had expected. Over the years, he was often out at night, playing the sax in local bands. Sometimes I thought he did it just to get out of the house.

Along the way, I became involved with recreational drug use. It started out back in the eighties; that's what people did recreationally. And if you thought you were part of the "in crowd," you did that. That was my choice. No one led me down a dark path or anything. I was a willing participant, and it got out of hand. Eventually, I was getting high to cope with stress. I smoked marijuana. I snorted coke. Basically, I was a functioning addict: I worked my job. I took care of the kids. And at night I would get high.

That went on for about ten years. I was very careful about keeping the drug use away from the kids. From the outside, we looked like the perfect little family. We had two beautiful kids, we lived in nice places, and we had good jobs. And I was high almost every night.

Momma knew about the drugs. She didn't know to what extent I was involved, but she knew. And she always made a point of saying, "All right now, you need to slow down." She was always nonjudgmental, but worried nevertheless.

That was the thing about my momma: even when I wasn't doing right, she loved me. Even though I was messing up, getting high, trying to hang tight so on the surface things looked good, she stood by me. We had nice cars and we lived in nice houses and the kids always looked well-kept and all of that. But behind closed doors it was a damned mess. Momma knew all of that, yet every time I would go home and visit, she would always put some money in my hand and say, "Now this is for you. Don't let Bernard know you got this."

I knew things had to change. I was so tired of feeling useless. Our kids were growing up and I was trying to make sure they could be in all the activities and everything they wanted to be in. I wanted to be *present*—yet still trying to get high all in the mix. It was just a mess!

One Saturday, I had gotten high. I mean, just really high. When I woke up the next morning, something snapped in me. *I'm not doing this no more.* I told Bernard, "I gotta go to rehab. I gotta check myself in."

I called Momma, crying. "Momma, I think I'm having a nervous breakdown. I've got to check myself into rehab," and I hung up the phone.

And then I put myself in rehab. Because we had such good insurance through UPS, where Bernard worked, I was able to get into a good treatment program. That was the hardest thing I had ever done. I was locked behind doors in this little room, getting the drugs out of my system, taking vitamins, talking in group, and trying to figure things out.

Twenty-eight days I was in rehab. Twenty-eight days I was away from my kids, but they didn't know I went in rehab at the time. They just thought I'd had a nervous breakdown. That's what we were calling it. Brandon was twelve or thirteen at the time, and he would not come to see me. He did not want to see me there. Aja came and brought me Oreo cookies. I have a picture of the two of us there, and it still breaks my heart just to look at it.

One of the employees there was someone I had gone to college with. Can you imagine? The person was so very nice to me and did not make me feel bad. But I was so embarrassed.

So I got clean and went home—and I relapsed. I always wanted to put it on other people, but that was on me. That was me being weak. I would rationalize: *I might as well get high, 'cause nothing else is happening.* I just fell back into the old habits and went on living.

Bernard and I had married so young, before we really knew each other or ourselves, and then we jumped right into parenthood. We argued a lot. Finally, we separated in 1996.

Oh my, that was hard! I went to spend some time with Momma in Charleston. Aja came with me. She was twelve or so and Brandon was fifteen. He decided to stay with his father. It was hard leaving him behind, and it was hard going back to Charleston. There was something always suffocating to me about Charleston. I just never felt like I could breathe there.

I was mad at myself for having to go home to Momma, but of course she welcomed us. Still, it was a difficult time. She still saw me as a child. She tried to keep her opinions about Bernard and me and my choices to herself, but every so often she would just say, "When you get sick and tired of being sick and tired, you'll know."

Momma was the kind of person who—bless her heart—well, you weren't staying with Momma without pulling your share of the load. I found a little temp job. Meanwhile, Bernard and I were back and forth, with me being in Charleston with Aja and Brandon in Charlotte with him. I just got sick of it.

Aja really hated it in Charleston. She has her own stories of how Momma didn't really treat her well. I was working and hanging out with people I knew. I left Aja with Momma a lot when I should have been there with her. I don't know what was going on in my mind.

Aja started getting in trouble at school because she just didn't want to be there. And then she called Bernard. He came down and Aja packed her stuff up and went back to Charlotte with him.

I guess I stayed in Charleston for another week after that. I told Momma, "I've got to go home." I called Bernard and told I was coming back to Charlotte. "We're gonna work on this."

I didn't want my kids to have a broken home. My parents had stuck it out to raise us kids. They waited until we all left home before they separated. But Bernard and I got into a fight almost as soon as I came back to Charlotte.

It was my fault. I picked an argument with him while he was trying to get ready for work one morning, knowing full well it would make him volatile. I don't recall what we fought about that final time, but he shoved me against the wall. After he left for work, I called the sheriff and reported him for domestic abuse.

I orchestrated all of that, and that's something I regret more than I can say. People always say, "I have no regrets." Well, hell yeah, you have regrets. Everyone has things they regret. And I do regret that. I know it was wrong, but I didn't see any other way out. I didn't know how else to get out of the marriage. I just didn't know how to leave. I had just gotten back from Charleston. I didn't have a job, I didn't have a car, I didn't have a damned thing. I just knew I had to get out of that marriage.

When Bernard got home from work that night there was a deputy sheriff at the door telling him he needed to get what he could get now, because he couldn't come back in the house. It was close to Christmas. The kids were there and looking at me like I was crazy.

"Why are you doing this?" they wanted to know.

There was no way to let them know just how desperate I was. The look on my children's faces tore at my heart. I felt like such a failure! That was the worst Christmas we had ever had.

I really do hate to put all of our business out there like this. But I honestly believe that people need to know the truth. People go through all of this shit, and then they run around and act like they've never had challenges. But I want people to know, to really understand, that just because you have gone through all of this mess, it doesn't mean you can't come out on the other side. You can.

I knew I had to get myself together for the kids, so I entered another rehab program. My children needed me more than ever. My behavior weighed heavy on my heart, but God told me: "You can do better than this."

That year, I turned back to the church for real. Just like my momma had, I got Jesus. I had lost touch with my childhood enthusiasm for God over the years. Although Bernard and I had attended a United Methodist church, I believe we went because that's just what you did. Bernard's dad would ask all the time when we talked on Sundays, "Did you go to church today?"

Even before Bernard and I separated, my friend Anita had invited me to a small Presbyterian church where she was a member. I went with her and I felt the same warm embrace I had as a girl back in Charleston. I taught Sunday school classes. The kids attended church with me and participated in church activities. I became the president of the women's group. I started singing in the choir. Anyone who knows me knows I can't sing a damned lick. But I was in there rocking with them. And they were like, "Sharon, uh…"

And I was like, "Look, y'all don't own this choir. God owns this choir. And I'm singin' in the choir!" I never sang a solo, to be sure, but I can rock with everybody else in the altos. Most of all, I felt like I belonged there.

After I'd had the sheriff make Bernard move out, the pastor of that church knew I was looking for a job, and told me that the Presbytery, the regional office of the denomination in Charlotte, was looking for an administrative assistant. He thought I was right for that job. "I told them about you."

I went to that interview, and before I even had a chance to get home—I was catching the bus and there were no cell phones back then—there was a message on my answering machine saying that I had the job.

That's when things started to turn around for me. I felt like I was able to put my life back together.

The kids were living with me and they were angry with me. They blamed me for the separation. Brandon never really talked about it. He once told me that he just kept telling himself, "All I have to do now is graduate from high school and get to college—and I'll be out of here."

Aja very much resented me, and Bernard leveraged her disdain to get information about what I was doing and where I was going.

While I was working at the Presbytery, a minister, Dr. James Thomas, noticed me, and he kind of took me under his wing. "Girl, have you ever thought about the ministry?" he asked.

No, I have never thought about that. You grow up thinking that people who are preachers are all high and mighty. But I did start thinking about it after he mentioned it. Could God really be calling me into ministry, or was this just my ego?

Then, in 2002, Rev. James Lee came to town, recruiting for the Austin Presbyterian Theological Seminary in Texas. "Come check out my school," he suggested.

I accepted his offer and went to Austin for an all-expenses paid weekend. I loved the leafy, serene campus. My soul was saying, *Wow, this is the most peaceful place in the world.* But my brain was telling me: *You can't do this.*

Rev. Lee kept telling me, "Yes, you can."

And so I did. I applied for admission to the seminary, writing essays and gathering letters of recommendation. I still had my doubts, but God worked everything out. Every time I told myself I couldn't do it, God stood there in the door and said, "What now? Just do it."

I got a scholarship and financial aid, and I headed off to Texas. I felt like I was saving my very life. Rev. Lee became my mentor. God has always connected me with people who saw something in me, and Rev. Lee was one of them. I am forever grateful to Austin Theological Seminary for allowing me in and giving me a chance to turn my life around and use the God-given talents I'd had in me all along.

I never worked so hard for something in my life. I *struggled* through Greek and Hebrew. But four years after I enrolled, I graduated from the seminary in May 2007, with a master's degree in theology at age forty-nine.

Momma came to Texas for my graduation, and she was so proud. She had been skeptical when I first told her I was going to seminary. "Are you sure this is what you're supposed to be doing?"

You didn't play around with Momma when it came to church. But she knew that if I put my mind to something, I would do it. She was the one who taught me that I could.

I began training to work as a hospital chaplain. I thought I could put my life experience to use there, helping people deal with their own traumas. First, I got an internship at a Veteran's Affairs hospital, focusing on substance abuse and mental health. I understood addictive behavior since I had gone through it myself. I could speak to people "on the real."

I also began preaching at a church in Dallas. Again, I used my life experiences. I talked about how we must truly commit ourselves to the Lord—body, mind, and soul—in good times as well as bad. "After all, look where God has brought us from. Look at what God has brought us through."

In 2011, I flew home to Charleston to give a sermon at Nadine's wedding at Mother Emanuel Church. I was struggling financially, but I found the money to go. I had finished my chaplaincy residence and was trying to find a job.

Of course, I wanted to preach the best sermon I had ever delivered and make Momma proud. Well, I went into that church, and *I turned it out!* My momma sat in the front row, just crying and saying, "Hallelujah!" I knew then that she really understood my calling. I felt like the prodigal daughter who had come home.

Nadine's wedding was beautiful. I was very, very proud that she gave me the honor of officiating, along with the Reverend Clementa Pinckney. That meant the world to me.

That was the first time I met Rev. Pinckney (who later was killed with Momma at Emanuel). He was just so gracious to me. He wanted to make sure that everything was cool. He wanted to make sure that I did more of the worship. He wanted it to be special for me and for Nadine. This was his pulpit and he welcomed me right in. He was the one who actually signed the marriage certificate, but he let me participate right alongside him in the service.

I got ordained in 2009, and in 2012 I started working as a chaplain at Parkland Memorial Hospital in Dallas. I worked the second shift, from three in the afternoon to eleven at night, in the trauma unit. I saw so many things. I saw people broken so badly, I wondered how they would ever recover. I was there, holding their hands, listening to them, and praying with them.

My own family suffered another trauma in 2013 when my sister Terrie died of cancer. The tragedy took a toll on all of us, and tensions rose. People like to believe that tragedy will bring families closer, but often it pulls people apart.

I got upset because my sister Nadine did something I could not understand. She was in charge of putting together the funeral program, and she included photos of everyone in the family except for my kids. Whatever the reason, it hurt my feelings that my kids were left out.

After Terrie's funeral, I returned to Dallas, still grieving my sister's death and feeling lost. Terrie and I had always been so close because we had been in college together and lived together there. I thought a lot about my family, my sisters, and my parents. And with all the family turmoil, I felt like I finally needed to know the truth about my biological father.

I had tried to bring up the topic with Momma once when I was much younger, but I had never asked about my father outright. It was clear that she didn't want to talk about it. I remember hinting around about it in high school. She snapped: "I don't want to talk about it."

One Sunday I called Momma and asked the question that had followed me throughout my life. I sat at my dining room table and called her. "Momma, do you know who my father is?"

There was a long, pregnant pause. "I thought that I was gonna take this to my grave."

She told me something I could hardly wrap my head around. When she was fourteen, she worked in a furniture store. She had always been chunky and she looked older than she was, so she lied about her age to get that job. One day, the owner's son was there with two of his friends. He told her that she needed to go upstairs to get something. They followed her up there. They raped her.

Rape wasn't something you talked about in 1958, especially a black girl being raped by white men. She was afraid to tell her own momma. I was born of violence.

I could barely process what I heard. I didn't talk to my mom for a couple days after that, as I tried to digest the news. I wasn't really mad at her; she had clearly been through hell. But I did feel hurt and confused. I was fifty-six years old and had believed one thing for my whole life. Now I was hearing something completely different. I didn't know what was true anymore. My entire life was suddenly in question.

I had always thought my father was Puerto Rican, and it's possible that he was. My mom was in a relationship with a Puerto Rican man at the time of the rape. He could be my father. Or my father could be a white man—a rapist. I will never know.

I suppose Momma let people assume the Puerto Rican was the father because it was better to be painted as a floozy than to say you were raped.

I thought about how I was so light-skinned compared with my dark-skinned family. I remembered how the kids in grade school would call me "half-breed" or "half-white." It spurred a lot of fights. In high school, when I would introduce Terrie as my sister, kids would think I was making it up because she was so much darker. They'd say, "She ain't your sister. How can you say that?"

In the black community, when you're light-skinned, people assume you think you're better than them. Of course, I never thought that. But I always talked back if someone confronted me.

Processing what I learned about how I was conceived, I felt more left out than ever. I thought about the tensions with Nadine. Did she resent me because I was light skinned? My mind raced. But there was one thing I did not allow myself to think about—the violence against my mother. I did not want to put that image in my head. I didn't want to think about that, or about the fact that my father could be a cruel attacker.

I had so many questions. But I didn't dig in and ask more questions. I felt guilty for making Momma talk about it at all. I knew this was deeply painful and uncomfortable for her. I could not imagine what she had been through. In fact, I debated about whether or not to put this part of my story in this book, because it was her personal story, and one that she had kept to herself. But this is my life story, and I want to tell it like it is.

My daughter tells me sometimes, "Mom, I don't know why you continue to say you're black. You're biracial."

But I never see myself that way. I grew up black. I live black. I eat black. I speak black. I am black.

CHAPTER 5

Funerals

After two days of being "flatlined" by the shock and grief of Momma's death, I had to muster the strength to travel to Charleston for the funeral. *Get up, Sharon. Shit gotta be done. Get your shit together.* I finally took a shower.

I don't even remember who drove me to the airport, honestly. But I flew into Charlotte, where Brandon and Aja were waiting. There was no way in hell I was going into Charleston without my kids. That was the longest plane ride I've ever had in my life. Every other time I had flown home, except for Terrie's funeral, it had been for happy occasions. *This one* was the longest trip ever.

I don't remember who sat next to me, but I know I was really fidgety. I wanted to say, "You know, my mom just got killed." But how was I gonna just start talking about that to a stranger? I didn't say anything, but I sure wanted to. I was walking around in a fog and a bubble, doing what I could to get myself through it. *I gotta get to Charlotte. I gotta get to Aja and Brandon. If I can make it to Charlotte—if I can keep it together and get myself to Charlotte—then I'll be okay. I'll be with my children.*

I was feeling sick on that flight. I hadn't eaten anything that day; I hadn't slept much in days. I'd been drinking way too much coffee. My throat was scratchy because I must have smoked two packs of cigarettes a day. I was a mess, and I just needed to be with my kids.

I'm of the mindset that when you travel, you don't look like a slouch. But on that day, I didn't care what my hair looked like. I didn't put on lipstick. I was just *raw*.

Brandon and Aja were waiting for me when I got off the plane. I was never so glad to see them in my life. We just stood in the middle of the airport hugging and crying. It wasn't hysterical or anything. It was our private moment in that very public place; yet only we knew what was happening. If other people had been watching, they might have thought, "Oh, I wonder what's wrong with that family?"

There were no words passed. We didn't need any. We probably wouldn't have had any to say anyway.

We headed to Aja's house. My kids stopped on the way and got me some Bojangles® Chicken, telling me, "Ma, you gotta eat something. Just a little bit." They could see that I was a total wreck. They were my caregivers because I had nothing to give myself. "Momma, you need to rest. Tomorrow's gonna be a long day."

Brandon was living with his girlfriend, but he stuck around until they got me to agree to lie down. After Brandon left, Aja settled me into the guest bedroom. And she mothered me. Aja always calls herself my momma/daughter, my mother/daughter. Sometimes that gets to be really annoying. I feel like saying, "Well, hold up a minute. I'm the momma, though. You can't tell me what to do. I don't have to listen to you!" But thank God for Aja. That day and every day, I thank God for my daughter.

We didn't talk much the day I arrived. Brandon and Aja just kept urging me to lie down because they knew I had not been sleeping. If I could get some rest, there would be a little calm. If I stayed awake, I wouldn't do nothing but sit there and talk—talk about Momma, and, "How could this happen?!"—and then we'd start crying again. Life was in total chaos and we just didn't really know what to say anyway. Whenever we talked, it was just so unbelievable, so surreal. But we had stuff to do. We had to get to Charleston.

My kids were worried about me, and I feel bad that they repressed some of their own stuff because they felt like they had to take care of me.

The next day, we drove to Charleston.

I was still in a fog. *How could this be happening? Were we really waiting for my mother's body to be released from the coroner?*

Under that cloud of sadness and stress, family tensions refueled.

We checked into a hotel and then went to Nadine's house. The press was on her because she'd been the one that on TV saying, "I forgive you."

And oh my God, the press ran with that story! *TIME* magazine did a big article on that and implied that Nadine and I were at odds because she forgave Momma's killer and I didn't. But it wasn't about that at all. The tensions between us had come from the fight we'd had after Terrie's funeral, long before. Momma's death just made it all very public. But that night, anyway, everyone was civil because we all were still in shock.

The following Monday, there was a meeting at the library for the victims' families and people from the church. They were trying to figure out how to schedule all of the funerals. They did not want any funeral held in the church before the pastor's service. Then we could schedule the other funerals. They were willing to do two a day to accommodate everyone, if they had to, but Rev. Clementa Pinckney's funeral would be the first at Emanuel.

Well, Nadine got belligerent, and the next thing we knew, Momma's funeral was going to be at Royal Missionary Baptist Church. By then, I'm guessing, Nadine had already talked to people at Royal Baptist. She didn't want to wait because she already had set things in motion. So when the Emanuel families said, "Let's get together and set a schedule," and wanted to wait until after Rev. Pinckney's funeral, she raised a fuss and stormed out of the meeting.

That same day, Nadine's daughter, Nadhina, and Esther's son, JonQuil, got into a scuffle. There was so much tension in the air. It didn't take much for tempers to explode.

I twisted my ankle trying to break up the fight. Actually, it was a hairline fracture, but I didn't realize it at the time. There was too much stuff going on for me to pay attention to the pain. I didn't even seek medical help until I got back to Dallas.

Nadine had already chosen the Palmetto Funeral Home. We all met there to plan the funeral arrangements. Nadine had already contacted Royal Baptist Church and decided that the funeral was going to be on Thursday, so I just went with that. I was just in no frame of mind to fight her every step of the way.

"Well, are you gonna do Mama's eulogy?" Nadine asked.

"No, I'm not gonna do Mama's eulogy!" I was in no shape to do that.

"Okay," she said. "I'll just get the pastor of Royal Baptist to do it." Royal Baptist was not a church to sneeze at. But it wasn't Emanuel.

I asked for the pastor's name so I could talk to him about the service. He was in Detroit and had no idea that he was supposed to officiate Momma's service. So no, he wasn't doing the eulogy. *You already got all of this planned, Nadine, but you ain't got a damned thing planned.*

There's a certain protocol in the African Methodist Episcopal Church. As a seminary-trained minister, I knew the funeral format for the AME Church. I just had to figure out who would deliver Mama's eulogy.

Somebody from Al Sharpton's camp called. "Rev. Sharpton will donate his time. He will do the eulogy for your mom."

What? "No! I appreciate the offer, but no." At that time he had his own political agenda, and we were not having that at Momma's funeral.

I called Rev. Novelle Goff, presiding elder at Emanuel. In the absence of a pastor, the presiding elder's job in the AME Church is to shepherd the congregation until they figure out who to call as the next pastor. So Presiding Elder Goff was running the show. I called and told him what was going on. He was emphatic: "Miss Lance is not going out like that, with a stranger performing her service. I will preach her eulogy."

Then we had to schedule the repast. Nadine said that the repast would be at Royal Baptist Church, and they wanted three thousand dollars to feed three hundred people. That was Nadine's guess on how many would come for the repast. "We don't have this kind of money," I reminded her. Later, the city of Charleston decided to reimburse us for the funeral, but at that time I was trying to plan things based on what we could afford.

Rev. Goff stepped in again. "Don't you worry. You just plan." Emanuel AME Church paid for the repast.

Momma was the first of the nine victims to be buried. She was laid to rest on June 25. It was one of those days in Charleston—muggy and sunny and hot. The limo picked us up at the hotel and took us to a parking lot in North Charleston to assemble for the procession. It was a very long procession, with people and cameras everywhere.

Even on the day of the funeral, all of us were separated. We all walked in separately. The order of the processional in the Black Church is very important. Who's in the front? That's a big question. I was in the front because I was the oldest. Esther and Gary were with me and my kids. Nadine and her entourage came in behind us. They seated us first, and Nadine walked by. To have my sister just walk by me—no acknowledgment, no nothing—was so painful. We were so disjointed. Even at Momma's funeral, the lines were drawn. It was like we were part of a bad movie. I'm sure that the people who knew our family could tell that something strange was going on.

The church was full to the rafters. Gov. Nikki Haley was there. Charleston mayor Joseph P. Riley was there, along with Revs. Al Sharpton and Jesse Jackson. It was a media event. There were cameras inside, and media outside. *If we have to bury Momma, it should've been at Emanuel.* Her funeral probably would have had a good turnout under normal circumstances, but this was beyond my imagination.

The service felt very impersonal, in a way, with so many people there and all the media and cameras. But Rev. Goff and I had planned things, and I tried to make it as personal as I could. I asked my mom's longtime hair stylist, Rev. Cecily Brown, to read Scripture. Both of my children spoke about Momma. JonQuil wrote a freestyle piece about her, and Najee, Terrie's daughter, got up and talked too. After Terrie died, Najee lived with Momma when she was home from college, and Momma had practically raised Najee anyway.

We sang one of Momma's favorite songs, "One Day at a Time, Sweet Jesus." Momma was like me: we really couldn't sing, but we sure sang a lot!

Crystal Brown, one of the musicians from Emanuel, sang Gladys Knight's "You're the Best Thing That Ever Happened to Me." We sing that as a gospel song in the Black Church, and, oh, did Crystal sing that song. It was beautiful.

Some family members were hollering and going on during the service. It was like a sideshow with all of that crying and hollering. I didn't want it to be like that, and I knew Momma would want us to be dignified.

Bernard, my ex, was very supportive. We sat next to each other, and he kept telling me, "Sit up. Put your head up." I wanted to fall apart and scream and holler like everybody else. But he was like, "Nope, nope, nope. Sit up. I got you."

I held JonQuil's son during the service, and someone took a picture of us that was printed in the newspaper. I see that picture now and I think how right it was to be holding him. Momma didn't get to see Junior before she died, but holding onto that baby at her funeral felt like affirming new life.

Poor Esther got sick in the midst of the funeral. She went outside to lie down in the limousine, so she missed most of the services. Even at the graveyard, she laid in the car. She didn't get out, and I think she carried some guilt about that for the rest of her life.

After the service was over, we drove to the cemetery. People were *everywhere*. The family sat under a tent. We released doves, and it was beautiful. It cost more money to have the doves. I worried about the money, but we felt like Momma deserved doves. The graveside service was no longer than twenty minutes, but oh, it was hard.

We had the repast at Royal Baptist Church, and it was beautiful. They had just finished their new education building and fellowship hall. They hadn't even opened it yet, but they allowed us in.

The church had their own caterers, so we just went with that because it made things much easier—and the food was good. I didn't really eat, but I knew we had to have chicken and red rice. It's red with tomato paste and tomato sauce, and a staple in Charleston's African American community. We probably had macaroni and cheese and string beans and corn, cakes and desserts, cobblers and all the things they usually serve at a repast. There was plenty of food.

At the repast, we started to have conversations and greet the people that we'd missed at the funeral. Still, I don't remember seeing a lot of the people I know were there. I walked around and greeted as many people as I could, thanking people—including Momma's half-sisters and brothers—for coming.

My mother was an only child, and an "outside" child. Her biological father had another family, but she had half-brothers and sisters. When she became an adult, she was finally acknowledged as Freddy Mack's daughter and his children started to welcome her into the fold.

I don't think any of the other victims' family members came, because everybody was dealing with their own stuff. I don't blame them at all. The only funeral I went to besides Momma's was Rev. Pinckney's.

Family sides were taken even at the repast. So on the day we buried my mother, I felt like I hadn't just lost Momma, I had lost half my family.

Rev. Pinckney's funeral was the next day. The service was held at the College of Charleston because so many people wanted to attend.

I had a black and white polka-dot dress that Momma had bought me for my seminary graduation. While I was packing in Dallas, I grabbed that dress and threw it in the bag, along with other random items thinking, *Whatever else I forgot, whatever else I need, I'll buy it when I get there.* I bought a new dress for Momma's funeral, but I wore the dress she had bought me to Rev. Pinckney's funeral. That's what I was wearing when I met President Obama, so it felt like she was with me there.

We all were just emotionally wrung out. My daughter Aja didn't want to go. She couldn't handle another funeral and all of the crowds. Brandon and I went and found ourselves in a sea of people.

There was some miscommunication that morning about the time we were to meet at the church to go to the college. When we got to Emanuel, people were everywhere and we got stuck in that huge crowd. As I scanned this mass of humanity, I thought: *You know what? Somebody is gonna get us to this College of Charleston, because I am not about to walk through this crowd! We are members of the family, and we need to be there to represent Momma.*

My foot was hurting pretty badly by then (from my earlier ankle injury), but I was determined to attend the service.

I walked up to a uniformed gentleman. "Sir, I'm Sharon Risher. My mother was Ethel Lance. We buried her yesterday. I need to get to the College of Charleston and I can't walk."

They put us in one of those little golf carts. My son was like, "Ma, you can't..."

"Brandon, come on!"

They drove us to the college and we were escorted to the area where we needed to be.

It was overwhelming. People were *everywhere*. Cops and people in uniform were everywhere. Security was tight, and you needed a special wristband to be seated. There was a designated section to seat the family members of victims.

We were really close to the stage, but off to the side in a balcony-type section. The mayor and all the other dignitaries were seated on the floor.

Electricity was in the air, and people were abuzz. It was an odd mix of emotions— anticipation, the sadness of having just buried Momma, the energy of President of the United States being in attendance—it was just surreal.

All I could do was cry. The whole time. I had made up my mind that this was the only other funeral I would attend. I was gonna pay my respects to Rev. Pinckney, but emotionally, I just couldn't do anybody else's. Not Cousin Susie's, not even Myra's. I just couldn't. Everybody kind of did that. They didn't worry about attending other funerals because everybody was so distraught about their own loss.

The AME Church knows how to do pomp and circumstance. All the bishops were on stage, and so many dignitaries were there. It was very much an AME-type of service, but on steroids.

People were everywhere. There was a buzz like—oh my God!—all these voices and people. When President Obama stood and started delivering the eulogy, I was close enough to feel him choking up. His face started to glisten. He talked about gun control, ending poverty, and racism. He *preached!*

The whole time I sat there crying I was still beaming, because I was in the presence of the first black president. I thought about how proud Momma was when she voted for him. Momma *always* voted. She never took that right for granted.

Momma, look! Your boy, President Obama, is here.

After a very pregnant pause, President Obama started singing "Amazing Grace." All of the bishops and everybody in the audience stood and started singing with him. It was so beautiful—like a dream that leaves you feeling good.

There was lots of singing at that service, and lots of people talking about Rev. Clementa Pinckney. It was all very nice, but the thing that stood out for me, and still stands out now, was President Obama singing "Amazing Grace." He barely made it through, but he did. He didn't care how he was going to sound; it just came out of his heart.

I felt so proud that the first African American President—as busy as he was, and even though this was a horrific thing—let nothing keep him away from being there. *Momma, look at all that's happening.*

After the service, they escorted all of the families to a place to meet with President and First Lady Michelle Obama. They had cordoned off a space for each family, with chairs and a little bit of privacy.

The Obamas went to each family's cubicle to meet with them. Finally, they came to ours—Brandon, Nadine, Najee, and me. When President Obama walked in, I felt my knees go week. *Oh my God, I am standing in front of the President!*

He and Michelle introduced themselves and started hugging people. At first, I extended my hand because I wasn't sure of the protocol, but President Obama just grabbed me in this hug that was chest to chest. I could feel his heartbeat—*that* close. I was feeling joy and pride and sadness, all at the same time. *Momma, can you imagine? Can you imagine, Momma, that we are hugging President Obama? Because of you, Momma. Because of you.*

And that's the way I look at all of these things. Momma always kind of wanted to stay in the background, and look what happened because of her. I thought about how Momma would have given her left eye to meet President Obama. And here I was, standing next to him, because of her. It was all too much to grasp.

With him holding the highest office in the United States, you might think he would be a little standoffish. But no, he was very approachable. And he smelled so good! I never smelled a man that smelled like that in my life! I get that very much from my momma: I love a good fragrance. His cologne wasn't overpowering. I don't know what brand it was; I wish I did. But it was just like—well, I imagine God must smell like Barack Obama. He and the First Lady were both so kind to us.

He asked us if there was one thing his administration could do, what would it be. Nadine talked about getting something for the kids in the schools. Brandon talked about mental health care. He works in mental healthcare.

Mr. Obama listened to us and he said, "It's great to hear what you have to say." He didn't try to make any promises. He just listened.

They stayed with us for a good twenty or so minutes, and then moved on to meet other families. After meeting him, I knew that he was for real and that he was a man who really cared. Since the most recent presidential election, I have thought many times, *If this thing had happened during the Trump administration, Lord have mercy. Can you imagine?* I think the murders would have meant nothing to him.

Before they left, one of the president's staffers gave me his business card and said, "Ms. Risher, if our administration can do anything for you, here's my card. All you have to do is send me an email."

I don't know who he was. I remember his first name was Barry. The card is buried somewhere in my storage unit. Everything I packed when I left Dallas in 2016 is still in a storage unit three years later.

I do treasure the picture of us with the Obamas. Nadine and Najee were beside Michelle, and Brandon and I were beside the president. I never put that picture out because my daughter was not there. I just didn't feel complete putting that picture on Facebook or even displaying it, because Aja was missing.

After the funerals—Momma's on Thursday and Rev. Pinckney's on Friday—it was Father's Day weekend. Bernard was still with us in Charleston, so we had a really nice Father's Day dinner with Bernard at one of the waterfront restaurants.

On Monday, we checked out of the hotel and drove back to Charlotte. It was time to go home and begin picking up the pieces.

CHAPTER 6

A New Normal?

When I got back to Dallas, I could not get back on my feet—literally. I had broken my ankle while trying to break up that scuffle in Charleston. Adding to my struggles was the fact that my colleagues at the hospital were not very understanding about the fact that I needed to take some time off to recuperate. They were eager for me to come back full steam. My boss called several times, asking when I was coming back.

Can you not understand what I have been through? My momma just got murdered in a church. It's not like she died of natural causes. We are chaplains. We care for people who are hurting when they come to the hospital, but you can't care for one of your own?

Later I wrestled with whether I judged the hospital too harshly then, but in my heart I couldn't reconcile how I felt at the time. I loved serving at Parkland. I was a team player and worked hard to enhance a good, solid pastoral care department. I worked with some amazing chaplains. My girl, Janie Delgardo, kept that department in check on the administrative side. We formed a friendship that I will always cherish. The doctors and nurses, everyone who served day after day in the emergency room where I served, and especially the workers who kept that hospital clean, all were good and compassionate people who took pride in their work. We served the Dallas County Hospital District with pride.

"Every man for himself, and God for us all." I thought all the time about Momma and the phrase she was fond of quoting. I thought about her describing a new perfume she wanted during our last conversation. "Ooh, I smelled this Banana Republic perfume. I sure would like to have some of that."

"Ma, would you like me to buy you that perfume?" I bought it for her, but I didn't send it right away. That bottle of perfume was delivered to Momma's house the day after she died, and that haunted me.

I felt guilt. I couldn't sleep. I couldn't eat. My doctor prescribed sleeping pills just to get me by. I felt guilty that I wasn't in Charleston when it happened. I wasn't there during all of the chaos and everything that followed—not being at the church after the massacre, and then at the Embassy Suites waiting to hear news in the aftermath.

I felt I should have been there. My logical mind reminded me that there were other family members who also weren't in the city at the time. They were a long way off when it happened, too, but it still bothers me a lot that I wasn't there.

Not long after I got back to Dallas, I got a package of cards and letters from Emanuel. People from all over the country were sending notes, and the church was forwarding them along to the families. One envelope had my name written on it. I opened it and read the most heart-wrenching letter from a woman named Lucy McBath. I searched her name on Google and found out that her teenage son, Jordan Davis, had been killed in Jacksonville, Florida, on the Friday after Thanksgiving 2012. He and his friends were at a gas station playing loud music in their car. A 47-year-old white man named Michael Dunn shot into the car and killed Jordan. It was just senseless.

Lucy just poured her out heart about losing Jordan. She understood my pain and wanted me to know that there was a group of people who understood what it meant to be a gun violence survivor. She included her phone number in the letter, "You call me any time." I called her immediately.

We talked and cried and then cried some more. Lucy listened as I poured out my heart. She told me that we shared a pain that other people will never be able to understand. Then she gently told me about the "Everytown for Gun Safety" survivors' network and the work they were doing to enact commonsense gun laws and to help end gun violence.

When I got off the phone, I sat on the couch, thinking about the conversation and wondering if I should get involved somehow. I had finally gone back to work, just after my birthday on July 10, so no way did I have time for that.

It was a really busy time at work. The hospital was preparing for a move to a new facility across the street. But when the time came to move patients across the bridge to the new building, all I could do was sit and watch, because of my ankle.

On July 24, I got a phone call from the folks at Everytown, inviting me to come to Washington, D.C., and participate in a call to action on Capitol Hill—all expenses paid. The staff would take care of everything. *Oh shit, they want me?* I couldn't believe this was happening.

I knew my boss wouldn't approve me taking time off from work to attend. I had a decision to make. I didn't want to lose my job, but the tiny, powerful echo of God inside me said, *Do it. Do it.*

So I did it. On July 28, I was on Capitol Hill with people from "Everytown" and "Moms Demand Action for Gun Sense" in America. Senators Chuck Schumer, Chris Murphy, and Richard Blumenthal joined us to demand a vote from Congress on saving background check legislation to keep guns out of the hands of dangerous people.

Survivors of gun violence were there from all over the country. I met Sandy Phillips, whose daughter Jessica was killed in the movie theater mass shooting in Aurora, Colorado, and Richard Martinez, whose son Christopher was shot in May 2013 near UC Santa Barbara. I also met Shannon Watts, who had been a stay-at-home mom just doing her thing until the Sandy Hook Elementary shootings. The next day, she started a Facebook group to talk about gun violence. That group grew into Moms Demand Action for Gun Sense in America.

I just couldn't believe that I was standing there with these people. And because of what happened in Charleston, I was about to get up in front of all these people and say something. My adrenaline was pumping, and I was scared. I didn't want to sound like a blubbering idiot. It had only been a month since Momma was killed and I was still very emotional.

God, please don't let me have a meltdown! That's still my prayer every time I get up to speak about the Charleston shootings. Sometimes I cry harder than at other times, but I'm always able to get up and speak.

I drew on my training as a pastor. I know how to preach, but I don't think I even knew what I was doing that day. The folks from Everytown helped me construct my words, and I spoke my truth.

Being with other survivors was very affirming and empowering. It was also very emotional. I felt like I was part of something bigger then myself. Then, it was time to go home again.

I loved my job as a chaplain, and I was good at it too. A hospital chaplain has to be calm, although sometimes I would cry harder than the people I was trying to help, especially when young kids were involved. I saw so many things in that intensive care unit. I saw people with their bones poking out of their skin. I saw people burned so badly you could smell their charred flesh. I saw a mother whose baby had died of smoke inhalation. When she learned her baby was gone, she released a primal scream, and I thought I was gonna melt through the floor.

But as a chaplain, you're there to help, so you hold their hands, you whisper in a grieving ear. You try to help them get through the trauma in any way you can with God's help. I loved being a comfort to people, even if only in a small way, during the most trying times of their lives.

One time, a young white woman in her early twenties came to the emergency room. She looked like she had not had an easy life. She had been sexually assaulted, and she was bruised and clearly traumatized. She didn't want to talk to the rape counselor. She didn't want to take off her clothes and do a rape kit. I needed to try and soothe this young sexual-assault victim, to help her come to a quiet place and rest.

As a chaplain, sometimes you have to be vulnerable. Yes, you have the authoritative titles of "Reverend" and "Chaplain," but you need to be a *real* person to make people feel safe. Sometimes you have to disclose personal details to make people comfortable. I wanted this young woman to know that her world was not over and that she could survive. This event need not define her or tear her life apart. I confided that my mother had survived a violent rape and had gone on to raise a family and lead a fulfilling life.

I believe that sharing my mother's experience helped her, because, eventually, the young woman did calm down. She agreed to talk to the rape counselor and move forward with the rape kit. I told her to come back one day and look me up. Occasionally people would come back later to say hello and let me know how they were doing. I never saw that young woman again, but I hope the story of my momma and me helped bring her some comfort on that stormy night.

I'd dealt with many challenging life situations, but Momma's death was putting my faith to the test in a way more profound than ever before. Sometimes I prayed hard, and other times I couldn't pray at all. For a time, I stopped going to church. I just felt overwhelmed. I knew in my heart and in my head that I would return to church someday, because I had no choice. But I just kept wondering, *Why, God? Why?*

The day after the shooting, the pastor at my church showed up at my door with the bishop. They prayed with me and did what they were supposed to do. But after I got back to Dallas, I felt very much alone.

Every now and then, one of the church members would call. Maybe they didn't know what to do or say, so they just kind of left it alone.

After Momma died, I just needed some time to grieve, so I didn't go to church a lot. I just didn't want to be in church. I didn't want people to feel sorry for me. I didn't want people to have to look at me and figure out what to say.

I looked at church online. That's how I became friends with Rev. Dr. Michael Waters, a young AME pastor who graduated from Southern Methodist University. Mike's church broadcasts their service online. Mike became my personal pastor. He made time for me to call him and cry, and he would just listen.

Sometimes I would watch Bishop T. D. Jakes. I listened to gospel music. I read the Bible. It was like I had my own church. I didn't have to be in a church building to know God and worship Him.

I didn't want to be around church people. I didn't want to be sitting in a church. I still believed, I just didn't feel connected. Even in the midst of reading Scripture and listening to gospel music, there still was a kind of disconnect.

I talked to my kids and to my sister Esther all the time. I talked to the other families who had lost loved ones at Mother Emanuel. Ultimately, because of my faith and the faith of the people in that church, I was able to continue getting out of bed. I always knew Jesus Christ would strengthen me and give me what I needed to carry on.

I was in Dallas the day the Confederate flag came down from the capitol in South Carolina. That symbol of hatred flew over my head every day as a child. Not quite a month after the Emanuel shootings, the flag came down on the blood of those nine people who were killed. *Okay, Momma, what a wonderful birthday present you gave me. Look at what you have helped make happen. It's because of you, Momma.*

Before Gov. Haley orchestrated the flag's removal, I hadn't given a whole lot of thought to the Confederate flag; I just knew it was something that should not have been up there. We had reached a point in America when that symbol just wasn't cutting it anymore. When that flag came down, I felt a wave of peace. Momma helped get that done.

I was proud of the fact that even in her death Momma had helped cause this to happen. But then I got to thinking about the other side of that coin, knowing South Carolina politics as I do. *Mmm-hmm. That was a token to Charleston and the people of South Carolina that, "Yes, we can take down this thing."*

Nobody besides black people, I guess, felt like it was a flag of oppression. It seemed like nobody else could see that. They say it's history and all that, but from my African American context, it's oppression.

So I thank South Carolina for taking the flag down...*finally*. It took the murder of nine people by a white supremacist to make it happen, but I'm still grateful.

I don't live in Charleston anymore, so I can't say I've seen a lot of change since the flag came down. But Charleston is in a wacky kind of tourism blitz—lots and lots tourists—and Emanuel church is definitely a part of the "Charleston tour" now. So many people want to have a picture taken in front of the church. Sometimes I wonder if that church just needs to become a museum and get it over with. So much has gone on in the name of that church that I wonder if the spirit of that church will ever be the same. Blood was spilled in that church, and then people used the murder of those nine people for gain.

In a way, the shootings split the church the same way Momma's death split my family. There were a lot of questions about how the church collected and disbursed the money that came in. Cynthia Hurd's husband filed a lawsuit in order for to get the church to open the financial records. The fact that Steve Hurd had to go such lengths to get the church to open up about the money and how it was being spent was just crazy. It was a mess!

The church definitely gained monetarily from what happened. Emanuel has become a tourist site, and the monetary gifts to the church have definitely increased their finances. A number of documentaries also have been made about the place where those nine people were killed.

But victims' family members were feeling as if the church had disrespected them in a way. It felt like the church had its own agenda, and we were just a part of that. Whatever the church staff decided they wanted to do, they did, and it felt disrespectful somehow. They were making things and building things on the backs of the nine people who died in that church.

I know there was a lot going on, but there were no pastoral visits from the church to the different families that I know of. The church staff said they made telephone calls. I think Rev. Goff may have visited Felicia Sanders, and there may have been a conversation with Nadine. I never received a personal call from anyone at the church.

Poor Felicia was in a world of her own. She lost her son and her aunt that night, and she survived the shooting only by lying on top of her granddaughter and pretending to be dead. But Felicia suffered because of what Emanuel did in the aftermath too. I'm not sure of the specifics, but she had several disagreements with the church. She just felt as if the church didn't respond the way they should have. She was wounded by that, so she left Emanuel.

Some families felt let down by the church, and some people left. But people still worship at Emanuel every Sunday. They still have Bible study and they still do ministry. Some of the money has been used to fund an Empowerment Center that offers counseling and support to the survivors and victims' families. In the aftermath, Esther was very much involved in the Empowerment Center, and it helped her a lot.

* * * * *

In March of 2016, I visited Charlotte for my son's thirty-fifth birthday. On the way to the airport, someone crashed into the Uber car that was transporting me. Since I needed to get to my son, I just called another car and kept going. When I returned to Dallas, my doctor told me to take a couple more weeks off, between the broken ankle and the car wreck. When I told my boss, she was not happy. "But we've been covering your shift!"

I felt like my brain exploded. Then, a calm came over me. "After prayerful consideration, I've decided to hand in my resignation."

I could just imagine Momma going nuts in heaven, jumping up and down, saying, "Girl, you gonna give up your good job?"

Yes. Yes, I am.

Aja visited me in August, and I was so glad to see her—my protector, my daughter, my mother all at the same time. My foot was still hurting, so we didn't do much, but I was so grateful to have her with me.

Then Esther came. I was worried about her getting to Dallas because she had never been on an airplane. The Dallas–Fort Worth Airport is crazy as hell, and big as hell. But she made it and she didn't get lost. It was so good to see her, but it was hard to see her skin-and-bones physique, because she had always been on the heavy side. She just looked sick. Still, she was so good for my soul. We laughed and cried together. Esther was so damned funny. One night while she was there, we went out for Chinese food, and we laughed about Momma taking her plastic bag to a buffet. On Saturday night, she cooked red rice with chicken, and, Lord, it was good!

On Momma's birthday, we tried not to be sad, but we were. We bought flowers, Momma's favorite carrot cake, and balloons. We sang "Happy Birthday" and released the balloons for Momma and for Terrie, whose birthday was September 5. I made Momma's pork roast and we had a good meal.

So much stuff continued to go on in Charleston. Momma's estate was a whole new battle. I didn't want to be the administrator, because I knew how much work that would be. Nadine didn't want me to be the administrator, so we agreed to get a special administrator for Momma's probate and estate. Actually, there wasn't a whole lot to the estate, because Momma didn't own a house. The Law Office of Laura Evans connected us with Laura Moore, a Charleston lawyer who does *pro bono* work.

Nadine and Najee had cleared out Momma's place. They just took what they wanted and put the rest of Momma's things in storage. They called Esther about six months later and told her, "This is where the rest of Momma's stuff is. If you want it, you need to pay the storage rental fee."

Esther paid the fee for a while, and when she couldn't anymore, I started paying it. But I was in Dallas, so I couldn't get there. She kept saying she was going to go through things, but she never did. I guess it was too hard for her. So I made up my mind, finally, that whatever was in that storage unit, we didn't need it because it was just the leftovers of everything they had already picked over.

Nadine and Najee distributed the last of Momma's things to some people in the family. Gary's daughter got a few things and Momma's aunts got some things, but Esther and I got nothing.

That December, we had a beautiful surprise. President Obama invited all of the Charleston victims' families to a party at the White House. Can you imagine?

On Friday, December 4, Esther and I were in the White House, and when President and Mrs. Obama came down the stairs, everybody seemed to be pushing to get up next to them. But I just stood there staring. I was still on a scooter at that time because of my ankle. When it came time to go downstairs to the reception, they put me in a private elevator. The man operating it said, "You know, this is the president's private elevator."

"Can I take a picture?" So I have a picture of me in the president's private elevator. *Oh my God. Oh my God! I'm in the White House!*

The reception was beautiful. They had jumbo shrimp and roast beef and just any kind of thing you could imagine. And the desserts, oh my God. The wine was flowing, and the room was beautiful, and there was the Lance family, mixing with all these big, important people.

The afternoon before the party, we got to visit the Justice Department and talk with Attorney General Loretta Lynch. Being at the Justice Department was intimidating. She wanted to give the surviving families her own stance on what she felt, and how the Justice Department was going to do everything in its power to make sure that we got justice and a fair trial. "This is not a part of who America is," she told us.

It was the experience of a lifetime going to the White House, but that first Christmas without Momma was really hard. I bought my children engraved watches to remember her by.

More than a year later, in May of 2016, I moved to Charlotte to live with my Aja—and to rest and heal a bit. I began speaking at various events and I met more famous people, such as filmmaker Spike Lee. I traveled to New York City for a feature story on Momma in *Marie Claire* magazine.

A new chapter of my life had begun.

CHAPTER 7

The Trial: A Sense of Duty

The trial *finally* began in December 2016, after several delays. All of us were anxious about the proceedings because we didn't know what we were about to face. I had to be there to represent Momma, even though I was not looking forward to sitting in the same room as the killer.

I made the trip to Charleston as if I were preparing for battle. I was going to do a job. So many thoughts were in my head: *I've got a job to do. I'm going to try not to be emotional. I know that I've got to keep myself together. I've got a job to do, and I'm gonna represent Momma. I don't care who else is there. It don't matter. I'm gonna be there for the duration because Momma deserved that.*

For a long time, I'd felt there was a dark cloud looming over Charleston. By the time I came back for the trial, I strongly felt that. Charleston represented oppression because it had always been a place where black people could not flourish. The only jobs blacks could get were in hotels and restaurants. So going back to that city for the trial of my mother's killer made me feel even worse about Charleston. *See, I knew!*

Back when I lived in Charlotte, I had selfishly tried to get Momma, Nadine, and everyone else to move there, too. "Charleston ain't got nothing going on. Ya'll should come here." Nobody ever moved, though.

See, I knew I couldn't stand this place for a reason.

The federal prosecution team, along with the federal victim crisis team, talked to the victims' families before the trial and prepared us for what to expect in the courtroom. They wanted us to be as comfortable as we could in such an uncomfortable situation. They also wanted us to know courtroom decorum was expected. No loud outbursts. No getting up and moving back and forth.

Okay, I'm getting ready to go into battle. I've gotta go into this place. I've gotta represent my Momma, just like I did at her funeral. That means I have to look right and have some decorum.

That first day in court, I made a note to myself: "I'm sitting in the courtroom not 15 feet away from 'him.' Today would have been Myra's birthday. Remember to call Denise."

Because it was such a small courtroom, they were very selective about who could be there. Only immediate family members of the victims were allowed in, and we all sat together. The press sat in the back row, but there weren't any cameras—just a courtroom artist.

Aja was able to stay by my side during the trial. Brandon came in, here and there, as much as he could. Esther and Gary came, and I made sure both had a ride to the courthouse. I called Esther most mornings to make sure that she was up.

Most of the time, Esther did not sit in the courtroom. I think it was just too hard for her. Most of the time, she sat in one of the many rooms in the courthouse reserved to accommodate family members that couldn't fit in the courtroom. Each room was equipped with a TV monitor, so family members could see everything that was going on. Every day, coffee, tea, and an assortment of snacks were made available in the rooms.

Chaplains were there every morning and, before the trial began each day, we had a group discussion about what had happened the day before and what was going to happen that day. We prayed together every single day.

I would be hearing all the terrible details of Momma's last moments of life, and how terrified she must have been. Momma was the last person killed in that room. She saw it all before she died.

When the killer was escorted into the courtroom, he never looked at us. He kept his head down and maintained a rigid posture throughout the proceedings. No movement. No sign of remorse. When I entered the courtroom for the first time and sat just fifteen feet from Dylann Roof, it felt like I was in the presence of pure evil.

When you're occupying a room with pure evil, you have to stand up on the inside, with your head held high.

Initially, the killer had tried to represent himself, but the judge made sure that his lawyers were there. From my understanding, he didn't want his attorneys to introduce his mental health history. His whole thing was stating he was *not* mentally ill. His lawyers had a hard time trying to defend that boy. Everybody already knew he had killed those nine people. They were just trying to keep him from the death penalty, and this boy fought them every which way but loose.

Is this fool gonna ask questions of the family members of the people that he killed? I felt so much anger at the thought. So much anger. *God damn this fool!*

One of the notes I made to myself during the trial reads, "I hate hearing his voice." Sitting so close to him, I kept trying to figure out why he did it. *What is in this little boy's soul?*

I sincerely believe he has mental health issues. I think he's had them all his life, and his family was in denial that something was wrong with him. I am not asserting that he shouldn't be held accountable for what he did. He murdered nine innocent people. But perhaps, had his issues been addressed when he was a child, he might have turned out differently.

The prosecutor, Assistant U.S. Attorney Jay Richardson, began by talking about each person killed. It was hard to hear him talk about Myra and my cousins. It was even harder to hear him talk about Momma.

Jennifer, Rev. Clementa Pinkney's wife, was the first to testify. She's a quiet, soft-spoken lady who was never involved in the way that one might expect of a first lady at a typical, big African American church. Often the first lady is very visible as the head of certain auxiliary boards, ministries, or other church programs. Jennifer wasn't that way, and that's probably what saved her life that night. She had come in the fellowship hall earlier to say hello to everyone, but then had retreated to the pastor's office with their daughter when Bible study began. She had some work to do, and she was helping their daughter with her homework. Jennifer heard the gunfire, moved to an adjoining office, locked the door, and she and her daughter crouched under a desk as shot after shot was fired. She heard the killer try to gain access to the locked office where she and their daughter were hiding before hearing him leave. Eventually, she managed to get to her phone and call 911.

How do you get the images of their bloody, broken, and lifeless bodies out of your mind? The pictures of the crime scene? On day three, we watched a video of the killer talking to FBI agents the day after the shootings. He actually laughed when he admitted he'd shot those people. When they shared Momma's autopsy report, and how many times she was hit by the bullets, my own body seemed to feel what Momma had felt. The things I heard and saw during the trial have left an imprint on my brain and on my soul that will forever remain. I sat there day after day, just feet away from the killer, trying to understand *why*.

He actually had visited the church three times before the shooting, scouting it out. When he arrived at Bible study that night, they welcomed him in. I can just picture Momma welcoming him, so proud of her church, telling him to come in and hear the word of God. He sat with them for almost an hour. Then, when they stood and bowed their heads to pray, he pulled out a semi-automatic weapon and started shooting. He pulled the trigger on his gun more than seventy-five times. He even stopped to reload.

He left three survivors in that room. My cousin, Felicia Sanders—whose son Tywanza and aunt, Susie Jackson, were murdered—survived by smearing blood all over her clothes and spreading herself over her eleven-year-old granddaughter and playing dead. She saved them both.

After he'd shot everyone else, the killer turned to Polly Sheppard. She was praying out loud and weeping.

"Shut up!" he said. "Have I shot you yet?"

"No," Miss Polly said.

This young man, so filled with evil, so filled with hate, told her, "Well, I won't shoot you, because I want you to tell the story."

The only other words he spoke during the entire shooting spree were to my twenty-six-year-old cousin Tywanza, who was trying protect his great-aunt.

"You don't have to do this," Tywanza told him.

"I have to do this, because y'all are raping our women and y'all are taking over the world," the killer responded.

When Momma was shot, her cell phone fell out of her pocket and slid across the floor. That's the phone Miss Polly used to call 911. Even in her death, Momma was still trying to help somebody.

I sat with the family members of the other victims. Listening to the details of what had happened to our loved ones, it felt as if scabs were being ripped from our bodies. We heard the terrible details of what had happened to our beloved. We saw the awful photos and every piece of evidence they had against this evil person. Lord, it was hard!

Sometimes it felt unbearable.

But if someone got overwhelmed with emotion, someone nearby would place a comforting hand on that person's back or someone in the next seat would extend a hand. We formed such a bond. Nobody's family was more important than anyone else's. We were in this together.

People have since asked me, "How could you sit so close to your mother's killer in the courtroom without screaming at him?"

But I *was* screaming at him—in my head. I sat there listening to everything while my brain was just screaming.

And sometimes, we got some needed comic relief. One day during the trial, Aja and I were sitting with Cousin Susie's family. We usually sat with them. Someone said, "If I was, like, a South American Indian, you know how they have those darts with the poison in them? If I had one of those, and I aimed it just right, I could take him out."

Finding humor helped us deal with the nervous energy we felt inside, trying to keep our heads cool. Aja had on some clunky heels. She took one shoe off, held it up and said, "Now if I aim this shoe just right, I could hit him upside his head."

That was some of the crazy, macabre humor that erupted from us being on edge every day, knowing just how close we were to the man who had killed our loved ones.

I forced myself to get up and go to court every single day—sitting in that stifling courtroom, reliving Momma's nightmarish death, telling myself, *Just hold on. Sharon. Just hold on. It's gonna be over with soon. You can go back to the hotel tonight. Then you can sit by the water and watch the boats.*

Our hotel was close to the marina, so every night after court, I would change into my casual clothes and walk to the waterfront. I'd spend my evenings leaning against the railing, watching the boats go by. The water was my solace. I would cry my heart out there and talk to Mama and get myself together. Then I'd go back to the room and get ready for the next day.

* * * * *

Dealing with the press was crazy during the trial. I had done some interviews previously, the first one right after the shootings. Brandon, Aja, and I, along with Depayne Middleton-Doctor's niece, were interviewed on *Good Morning America*. Then, a Dallas television station interviewed me on the day the Confederate flag came down in South Carolina. But once the trial commenced, we were on a whole different level of the media's radar.

Every day, the reporters were in our faces after court was dismissed. It's kind of intimidating to have people come up to you and stick a microphone in your face, because you have to talk off the top of your head and sound like you have some sense. I didn't want to come off as a stereotypical "angry black woman," but there was so much anger inside of me. *Okay, stay on task, Sharon. Try to answer these questions and let people know how hard this is, sitting through this trial. But this is necessary, and you're here for the duration.*

I learned to be selective about which reporters I would talk to. So many people were asking me to speak, and I just couldn't talk to them all. Sometimes I had to be firm in telling people no. They would call out to me, "Rev. Risher, just give me ten minutes."

"No. No. No."

Sometimes, I have to Google myself just to remember what I said to who. But I was there to represent Momma, and at some point I accepted the fact that I was going to be a part of the narrative.

* * * * *

When I was called to testify the first time, I spoke about Momma. I had prepared a written statement, but, when I got up to the stand, it was just overwhelming. I felt sick to my stomach, but I knew what I had to do. I was there because of a sense of duty—to represent Momma.

I talked about how Momma's murder had left our family in tattered pieces. The fabric of our family had been torn apart because Momma was the one who had held us together. I prayed that we would come back together and mend that tapestry, but how do you put back together something that has been ripped apart so violently?

I tried hard to hold it together and not to cry. I didn't want to break down on the stand.

I did not look at the killer during my testimony. There was no need for me to try to appeal to his heart. I fixed my gaze into the crowd and tried to stay focused. I just wanted to do what I was supposed to do.

After the shootings, I had to think seriously about capital punishment for the first time in my life. Before Momma's death, my belief pretty much was that anybody who killed kids or did something heinous deserved the death penalty. But before the trial, I started reading about the death penalty and prayed on it. I looked at the history of the death penalty and found out how many people—mostly black, by the way—had been put to death for things they didn't do. It shifted my thinking.

I knew Dylann Roof was guilty. Hell, he had laughed about killing my mother and the others. My angry heart wanted him dead, but my faith convictions took over and held firm to my heart and mind.

I hated even looking at that killer, but I don't believe we should take away someone else's life just because we have the power to do so.

Killing Dylann Roof was not going to bring my momma back. It wasn't going to bring my cousins back. Killing a killer wouldn't solve anything. *Besides, Momma wouldn't want this fool put to death.* That's how I have always thought of him. *This fool.*

After I finished testifying, I went back to my seat. My legs were shaking, and my stomach was churning, but I felt like I had done right by Momma.

All of the family members who were from out of town stayed at the Residence Inn, courtesy of the State Office of Victim's Assistance. They even let me bring my dog, Puff Daddy. It would have been a financial struggle to board him for that extended period of time. Plus, I needed Puff. He gave me something to worry about besides the trial. He also was my excuse to "pass" on some of those interview requests and return to the hotel as soon as court was over.

Thank God for Puff. I couldn't have asked for a better companion. He's old now, and his health isn't good. Sometimes I tell him, "Puff, you've done your job, Buddy-ro. You got Momma through a lot of stuff. And if you need to go, it's okay, because you've done your job."

There were always guards all around us at the hotel. We were well protected, and that was comforting. But the crazy thing was that the defense team was staying at the same hotel as victims' families.

One day, I was walking down the hall in the hotel when one of the defense lawyers approached me. I had been on CNN and all over the national news after I had testified, stating that I didn't believe in the death penalty.

"Rev. Risher, I just want you to know how much I appreciate your stance on the death penalty."

I looked at this man like he was crazy. *How dare you even approach me?* I did not respond, though. To me, he was representing evil, and I didn't want him to use my words to help that killer: "See? Even the families of the victims don't want the death penalty."

I didn't want to hear anything he had to say, so I just walked away. There was so much raw anger inside me during the trial, and it was very much on the surface of my emotions.

Later, I started having second thoughts on how I had reacted to him. *Now wait a minute, Sharon. You didn't have to be so rude.* I wasn't really rude. But I was very brusque with him because I was very hurt. *This man's just doing his job, and his client just happens to be this fool. So I don't have to feel like that toward him. This man is human just like me. He just happens to have this job.*

A woman on the defense team told me, "Rev. Risher, your testimony was so powerful."

Eventually I realized that the defense lawyers were doing their job to the best of their ability, but they had emotions too. They were reaching out to me as human beings—as people with hearts, not as people who were representing evil.

God works on you. He allows you to go through those human emotions. He knows you will come back to the spiritual side eventually, if you let Him direct you.

For so many days, I endured courtroom hell. The whole experience was like being in a damned movie—or one of the mystery books that I used to read. The courtroom air was filled with electricity, and I just kept looking at the jury. I searched their faces for some kind of emotion. I wanted them to look into my eyes and see my pain.

Part of me was afraid, though. I feared something insane might happen and they wouldn't find him guilty. You never know.

On December 15, the jury went into deliberations. Just two hours later we were called back in the courtroom to hear the verdict: "Guilty on all thirty-three counts."

Breathe, Sharon. Half of my brain was having a party while the other half was mired in sadness. I felt relief because, more than once, I have seen the judicial system be unfair to black Americans and people of color. The current political climate did not give me confidence in a system that has often failed African Americans. This was a victory, not only for the families and for black people, but also for the whole country.

When they announced those guilty verdicts, my brain had a party, with balloons and all kinds of craziness happening in there. Then, just as fast, I felt numb. Family members hugged and cried. We were so relieved.

After the verdict, I went back to Charlotte with Aja, drained by the whole courtroom experience. My energy level was low, and I was depressed. There were days afterward that I didn't want to put on clothes. I'd thought the second Christmas without Momma would be easier than the first, but it wasn't. I'm sure some of my sadness was part of the after-effects of the trial.

We tried to celebrate as best we could. Aja and I went to the mall and did a little shopping. We bought $46 worth of prime rib for Christmas dinner. My mental warning went out to the chef: *Better not mess this meat up.*

I thought about Christmas in 2012, the last time our whole family had been together for the holidays. Terrie was going downhill fast, and I had wanted to spend time with her before she died. We went to church together, and we all wore red and black. I don't remember why. We were still family then. We still had Momma holding us together. Even after Terrie was gone, we were still a family because of Momma.

It felt so strange that I couldn't ever talk to Momma again.

It was a very quiet Christmas.

In January, we were back in the courtroom for the sentencing phase. The prosecutors presented excerpts from a journal the killer had written in jail: "I would like to make it crystal clear. I do not regret what I did. I am not sorry. I have not shed a tear for the innocent people I killed."

No remorse. No regret. He even came to court wearing tennis shoes with racist symbols he'd drawn on them.

Family members were given an opportunity to make victim impact statements. Some powerful words were spoken.

Felicia Sanders—who had lost her son and her aunt in the shootings and had survived by playing dead and laying on top of her granddaughter—told him, "When I look at you, I just see somebody who is cold, who is lost...who the devil has come back to reclaim."

She was holding the Bible she'd had with her the night of the shootings. It was covered in blood. Felecia told him, "It reminds me of the blood Jesus shed for me and you, Dylann Roof... It will never lose its power."

She talked about not being able to pray with her eyes shut anymore. Every small sound scared her. "You are in my head all day." Then she said, "I feel sad for you. Yes, I forgive you. That was the *easiest* thing I had to do. But you can't help someone who don't want to help themselves... May God have mercy on your soul."

He never even looked at Felicia. He never looked at any of us. Not once.

Daniel Simmons, who lost his father, said, "You don't want to look at us... You don't have to look at me... God requires me to forgive you. He also requires me to plead and to pray for you."

Powerful testimony.

At one point, when Anthony Thompson was talking about losing his wife, Myra, the killer asked the judge to stop the testimony because it was "hurting his feelings." *Can you imagine?*

When my turn came, I said, "I pray those nine angels will visit you every night in your cell to have Bible study with you."

I looked at him. He didn't look back. I knew he wouldn't, but I also knew he heard every word I said. "And I pray that, before your life is over, you will call on the name of Jesus for mercy."

When the judge sent the jury to deliberate on his sentence, he instructed them that if they were not unanimous on the death penalty, the sentence would be life in prison without parole.

On January 10, we sat in the courtroom, waiting to hear whether his sentence would be life in prison without parole or the death penalty. The wait was agonizing. Esther wanted him dead. If I'm honest, there were times that I wanted him dead too. I wanted him gone from this earth. But then the Holy Spirit would bring me back to the spiritual person that I am. I couldn't stay in my humanness, because my faith and my heart tell me, "Thou shalt not kill." I seemed to be one of the few people who felt that way. Many people vehemently wanted him to get the death penalty.

My experiences have taught me that too many African Americans have been executed wrongly by the courts because of systemic racism. So I began to accept this movement of my emotions and feelings. I had to be willing to move like a ribbon of steel, fluidly, recognizing my humanness but staying in the spiritual. Otherwise, I would go down a dark hole, fully doubting my beliefs and weakening my faith.

My notes from court that day read: "Lord, your will is gonna be done. I will trust in the Lord because I can't do nothing else. Lord, you will continue to guide us all. Help us all to move towards healing. Less anger. Less family in-fighting. Finding a way to feel peace. It is well with my soul."

The jury returned. They didn't look at the killer, but some of them looked right at us family members. They recommended the death penalty.

At that announcement, we sat for a moment and looked at each other. We were just stunned, I guess. Then we all started hugging each other and crying.

The killer showed no response.

I'm so glad it was not left up to me to decide his fate. I thanked God for His grace and mercy. *Lord, I accept your judgment.*

I felt weak and nauseous. I was numb. Some of us just sat there, incredulous at what had just happened—justice for all nine of the people we loved. It was real.

Now that the trial was over, what was I going to do next?

CHAPTER 8

A New Ministry

Just a couple weeks after the trial ended, I was invited to speak at Limestone College in Gaffney, South Carolina, for their Martin Luther King Jr. Day observance. I had spoken on Capitol Hill twice, but Limestone was my first paid speaking engagement. There were probably three hundred or more people in attendance.

I was nervous when I wrote my speech, but I relied on my training as a preacher.

Esther and a friend of hers came from Charleston for the speech. Aja and my son's girlfriend were there, and Jennifer Berry Hawes, a reporter for Charleston's *Post and Courier* came. It was helpful to have family and friends there with me. I wore a green dress in Momma's honor, because that was her favorite color.

That speech was some kinda hard. My voice cracked. I talked about hearing Martin Luther King Jr. as a young child, and how that affected me. I shared how hearing him made me want to be a public speaker and a public servant, how I've always kind of known that's who I was.

I was really relieved when that speech was over.

After that, I began speaking more and granting interviews, writing articles, and speaking out against the death penalty. People apparently wanted to hear what I had to say.

My way of dealing with things is just to continue going. If I had let myself wallow, I might never have gotten back up. And why put yourself through that? Everyone flounders from time to time, but extended wallowing was an indulgence I didn't have time for.

There was a time before, though, during my marriage, when I *was* clinically depressed. I didn't seek treatment or anything for six months or so. I didn't want to go out of the house. I didn't work. I didn't do anything. Brandon, as little as he was, would make sure that I got up, cooked, and ate. I was a robot. I was ashamed of myself. I felt so hopeless, like I had no purpose.

Since that experience, I've determined that never again will I wallow like that, and that's where God and faith come into play. I don't ever have to go to that dark place again, because I've got too much to do.

I've been speaking at colleges and churches around the country ever since, and that has helped me to move forward. It is empowering and emotional, and I feel God's call to continue raising my voice for other victims of gun violence.

I still get nervous before television interviews. I try hard to make sure that what comes out of my mouth is true and authentic and that I'm answering questions intelligently. Black people often suffer from horrible image bias on TV—they opt to interview some poor woman with her hair all over her head, no teeth, trying to say something and making no sense. So my stance has always been that won't ever be me. I won't be on camera and not put together, and I work hard to string words together from my heart that make sense.

I think I've gotten the hang of doing interviews, and can get through them pretty well. When an interview is aired on TV, it is what it is. People will see it, but you seldom hear their comments about it. (Though, in this digital age, more and more, you can certainly *read* many of their comments online—if you so choose. I do not.) But what's especially scary for me is speaking in front of a group of people who have *paid* to hear me. When you're at the podium in a crowded auditorium, you get to look into people's eyes. Knowing that somebody has paid to have me there, I feel a sense of responsibility. I want to tell this story in a light that people understand Charleston wasn't just about the "news bites." These were *real* people, who left behind *real* family members who are still hurting.

Most of the time when I speak, there may be one or two hundred people in the audience—though, last year, at one of the colleges, we had a crowd of *eight or nine hundred*. That about blew me out of the water! I'm more nervous when the crowd is bigger; however, once I get to the podium and start speaking, I get into my zone and do what I do. When I finish, I look out at the crowd and see what's going on. Every time, it's like, *Wow*.

Sometimes are harder for me to speak about the shootings than others. And so many times I have wondered, *When will I ever stop crying?* Truthfully, I probably won't ever stop crying. My voice will probably always crack, especially when I call those names. Every time I speak, I call the names of the nine lives that were taken in that church, and my voice definitely cracks. Sometimes, my voice cracks through the whole presentation, and I remind myself that I'm not being weak. Sometimes, I can't help but to tear up or choke up, because that's the kind of story it is.

I've always been a communicator—a person who has something to say and has never been afraid to say it. Because of what happened in Charleston, I feel it's my duty to speak up for Momma and the others who were killed. God has appointed me to be one of the spokespersons for them all, so that America won't forget the nine lives lost through gun violence because of racism and hate.

Other Charleston survivors have been engaged in this struggle and accomplished some done good things. Rev. Anthony Thompson, Myra's husband, pastors an Episcopal church and had done some advocacy around gun violence. Daniel Simmons's granddaughter Alana started a 501(c)(3) called the "Hate Won't Win Movement, Inc." She's been going around speaking too. Felicia Sanders started the Tywanza Sanders Foundation in honor of her son.

We're moving in different circles, but everybody has their own niche. I took off on the gun violence issue because so many people have died because of guns, and I thought that it was important.

And I don't care who doesn't want to listen. I'm gonna keep talking as long as people keep inviting me to speak. The Charleston shootings made such a big impact in the media I keep getting invited to speak whenever the issue resurfaces on a national scale (which is— tragically—far, far too often). I've had innumerable opportunities to be on the national stage. I can't count how many events I've done with Everytown for Gun Safety. I can't tell you how much support I have gotten from others in that group.

Everytown is a grassroots advocacy group, educating and providing support to legislate commonsense gun laws. It brings survivors of gun violence together. Everytown was founded in 2014 by Michael Bloomberg as he was completing his final term as mayor of New York City. He donated $50 million dollars to start Everytown. He had just seen too much gun violence.

As I mentioned earlier, another similar group I've dealt with is Moms Demand Action for Gun Sense in America, which evolved after the shootings at Sandy Hook Elementary in Newtown, Connecticut, when Shannon Watts started an online chat about gun violence that grew into that organization she founded, Moms Demand Action for Gun Sense in America. Everytown and Moms have since merged efforts, though each group has kept its name.

I started out affiliating with Everytown because it was a place for survivors—helping people learn how to tell their stories and use those stories to push for commonsense gun laws. The people involved in Everytown became my lifeline. Losing a loved one in such a violent way cuts to the marrow of your bones, and being with people who know exactly what you are feeling is a great relief. There's nothing you can tell them that they haven't felt. That's a camaraderie that draws us together. It doesn't matter how it happened or whether it was race-related or not. Everytown unites people who have gone through the same kind of pain and grief.

My comrades in Everytown taught me that you don't have to feel bad about your grief and your anger. You don't have to be quiet about it, either.

Everytown has given me a platform to reach more people than I ever could have without them. Moreover, they have given me the confidence to use all of the skills and the faith that God has given me to reach people where they are.

I began finding my voice after my first speaking event with Everytown. Just three months after Momma's death, I had gone in Washington, D.C., for a second time to call on Congress to enact commonsense gun laws. I was still wearing a boot because of my broken ankle, so getting there wasn't easy. I needed my voice to be heard, and my trusty two-wheeled knee scooter saved me.

I stood before hundreds of people and I *preached,* but that was not the plan. I had planned to talk from my heart, and my message had been approved and edited by Everytown. But the spirit of God took control and led me to preach that day:

> There was gonna be nothing that was gonna keep me from being here today. In the days after my mother's death, nothing made sense to me. After such an action of violent hate, violence of racism, I knelt in prayer more than I ever have before. I was sure that God had forgotten me. It was like I was schizophrenic or something. I prayed constantly, or I didn't pray at all.
>
> My mother took care of that church to make sure that every corner, nook, and cranny was clean and available for all the worshipers to come in that house, just like the day Dylann Roof came with his racist thoughts and his racist heart, and he killed them all.

It's time to rise, people! To rise from Chattanooga, to rise from Lafayette, to rise from Roanoke, and to rise for the awful number of Americans who are killed by gun violence.

I'm asking the politicians here in D.C.: For whom do you stand?

Thoughts and prayers are not enough, people! When the vigils are over, when the candles stop burning, we need to stand up and say, "Whatever it takes, I am going to do it!" To God be the glory!

There have been so many opportunities for me to fulfill my mission through Everytown. In December 2015, I flew to New York City to film a public service announcement about gun violence. The NBA and filmmaker Spike Lee had partnered with Everytown to produce public service announcements that would debut on Christmas Day. NBA players and survivors like me were filmed talking about gun violence. I met Spike Lee at his New York studio to film that.

The next time I saw him was almost a year later, in August 2016. Spike Lee has a huge block party in Brooklyn every year on Michael Jackson's birthday. He had asked Lucy McBath to speak about gun violence, but she was not available, so they called me.

They flew me to New York and I stayed at a really nice Brooklyn hotel. That Saturday, the streets were blocked off, and people were everywhere. They had a stage set up and Spike Lee had a VIP tent where everyone waited for their turn to speak or perform. There was plenty of food and the drinks were flowing.

Fat Joe, a big-time rapper, was on stage doing his thing. When he finished his performance, it was my turn to speak. I don't know what got into my head. They must have thought I was Fat Joe II. "What's up, Brooklyn?" I hollered. You couldn't tell me that day that I was not a rock star.

For blocks and blocks, there was a sea of people. I was talking and people were actually listening. I talked about ending gun violence, and who I was, and what happened in that church to my Momma. When I finished, the applause was really overwhelming. When I came offstage, Spike Lee grabbed and hugged me.

* * * * *

A few months after Momma's death, I did a CNN interview with Brooke Baldwin about being a part of "The Loneliest Club," the club no one wants to be a part of. But there is also comfort in that club. There is always a bond among these people. You can reach out to them no matter what, and somebody is going to respond.

I've met people on this journey who are always going to be a part of my life—Lucy McBath, Shannon Watts, Chris Kocher from Everytown, and Dini Jones from Washington, D.C., whose daughter was gunned down outside of a party. She's still struggling with that, as any mother would. Then there's Judy and Wayne Richardson, a biracial couple from Maine whose daughter was killed in a home invasion. Judy and I are like sisters now.

We all share a common bond and a common goal—tell your personal story, how this has affected your life, and advocate for sensible gun laws so no one else has to join this club.

My work with Everytown is my ministry now, because one thing I know for sure is that the issues with guns are not going away. Plus, the reason why Momma and the others were killed in Charleston—racism—is not going away either. For me it's all tied up together. I'm determined to help America deal with these two critical issues in my own special way, from my own experiences.

My voice is necessary in this climate because I bring something unique to this movement—humor and willingness to be real. Sometimes people have a tendency to suppress things because they don't want to appear weak. My ability to be vulnerable is my connection point with people, along with my humor. If you can get somebody to laugh, even in the midst of craziness, that can help relieve some of the toxic anger that they carry.

People are living in fear and speaking out of their pain and confusion. It feels like we are living in a time when our country is divided more than it has been since the Civil War. People are being rounded up and deported. Families are being torn apart. It's a painful and confusing time filled with hatred and fear. And when guns are added into that mix, it gets deadly.

Gun violence touches every town and almost every person in one way or another. It keeps happening again and again and again. It almost seems like we've gotten desensitized to it—shootings in schools, shootings in churches, shootings in nightclubs. How many ordinary Americans have been killed just going about their daily lives?

I haven't gotten used to it, and I never want to, either. Every time there's another mass shooting, it takes me back to the night Momma was shot. *Every...single...time.* I turn off the television because I can't deal with it. I don't watch the news coverage of the shooting. I stay away from social media, because all day long that's all I would see and hear. I know the pain and grief these families will endure because their loved ones were killed by someone determined to bring destruction upon as many innocent people as possible. I know the chaos that is about to overtake their lives.

* * * * *

It's ironic how God can position people in your path to help you deal with your issues—whether you want to or not. In my travels, I became acquainted with Arno Michaelis, a former white supremacist. When he was a teenager living in Milwaukee, Arno was part of a skinhead organization.

Arno and I have the same booking agent, and we've done a few events together. I met him an event called "Living Legends" hosted by a Montville, New Jersey, middle school. The New Jersey schools host these programs every two years and bring in speakers from all over. You speak to all the kids in an assembly, and then go around the campus and speak to three or four classes.

At our introduction, Arno said, "Hey, I know who you are. My heart goes out to you." He seemed like a nice guy, so I went to hear him speak to one of the classes.

Arno started talking about his past. *You must be crazy if you think I'm gonna believe that you had this kind of hate in your heart, and then—all of a sudden—you don't anymore. You want me to believe that your life's work now is turning that around and helping other people out of the white supremacist movement?*

I was still carrying anger toward Dylann Roof, so I just didn't believe this dude talking about how his heart had changed. His message was compelling, but my heart just wouldn't let me let go there. *How do you even get there? Not that you even have the gumption to try and turn it around, but what made you even go there?* I brushed him off.

My first conversation with Arno was very tentative. This man could never understand the anger I held for his type of people. *How can people hate other people to such an extreme, simply because they are black, or Jewish, or gay?* He explained that Christian faith is one of the main things the white supremacist movement indoctrinates its members against. They are taught that the Bible is a fraud. So Dylann Roof believed attacking the church would send a big message. He wanted to mock the church and what it stands for.

Arno *was* interesting, and he seemed sincere. I enjoyed the dialogue with him, but I simply filed that encounter in my memory bank after we left.

Then, when I went to another Living Legend thing at Valley View Middle School in Watchung, New Jersey, Arno picked me up from the airport. "Hey, Sharon! How you doing?"

That ride gave me a chance to really talk with him. *You know what, Sharon? The same way that it took me a minute to forgive Dylann Roof, is the same kind of grace that I have to give Arno. Everybody can change.*

Arno explained how his transition started when he couldn't ignore the kindness shown to him by the very people he hated. He explained how he had been on a bender and had gone to work hungry. Everybody else was eating in the break room at lunch, but he had nothing to eat. A black man came over and gave him a sandwich.

After his daughter was born, Arno started distancing himself from the white supremacist movement because didn't want her to grow up in such hatred and violence. When she was ten, his daughter started reading a book by the Dalai Lama. He wanted to know what she was reading, so he read the book too, and eventually became a Buddhist.

Arno wrote a book after he left the white supremacist movement titled *My Life After Hate.* He was fairly well-known in Milwaukee by 2012, when white supremacist Wade Michael Page started shooting in a Sikh temple in Wisconsin. He killed six people and wounded four others before killing himself. Page had been a member of the same white power gang as Arno.

A son of one of the temple victims got in touch with Arno. Pardeep Singh Kaleka wanted to understand why someone would shoot people in a house of worship. Where did such hate come from? Pardeep invited Arno to become part of Serve 2 Unite, an organization that promotes tolerance and nonviolence. The two became really good friends and later wrote a book titled *The Gift of Our Wounds.* Friendship between a reformed skinhead and a Sikh Muslim is definitely *not* part of the white supremacist ideology!

Arno and I are friends now too. Who could have imagined that? I can talk with him and not worry about being careful about my words. My friendship with him and the testimony of his life are proof that anyone can change. In October 2018, we attended a Living Legends event in Central Valley, New York. Arno sent me a text message beforehand: "Your chauffeur awaits, Madam. I will see you in October."

* * * * *

One thing Arno taught me is how young men get drawn into the white supremacy movement, and the allure it has for people like Dylann Roof. When a young white boy's life hasn't turned out the way he wants, he feels like a loser and that nobody understands him. That's when the white supremacist ideology draws him in. They make him feel like he belongs. He becomes a part of a group—who also are losers. Collectively, though, they are not just a bunch of losers; now they have a common cause.

These people were waiting to receive Dylann Roof in when he ventured onto their racist websites. As a member of the white supremacy movement, he became somebody with an idea—and a gun.

But Arno is not on the gun violence circuit. He's on the anti-racism circuit.

There aren't many people working on the national stage who address the interface of gun violence and racism—the only ones I'm immediately aware of are Lucy McBath and me. Our stories got national attention because of the circumstances, but there are so many unheralded black people whose kids have been killed by gun violence. Those parents don't get the national stage, but a lot of background work comes from the Moms Demand Action chapters in cities across this country. Black moms are working hard in their own communities—hosting meetings, rallying, and canvassing—and they don't get paid a dime. They are the unsung heroes.

Prayers and vigils are not enough. As a person of faith, I do believe prayer moves things, so if all these people were actually praying, I think things might be different. But it also takes more than prayers to deal with guns. We need "prayers with feet." We need boots on the ground. God gives us prayer, but He also gives us the motivation, the intelligence, and the willingness to take action.

For too long, people in this country have felt powerless to confront the Washington gun lobbyists and the legislators who refuse to take commonsense steps toward reform. For too long the National Rifle Association has polluted our system with dirty money. Enough is enough!

Americans need to demand change from their representatives. Many people believe the gun violence in this country is not a political issue. Well I believe it *is* political; and, more than that, I believe it is a "heart condition." If gun violence in America does not make your heart hurt and cause pain in your soul, then nothing will.

Now is the time to get informed, to find out where your representatives stand on gun control, and to vote! When will we realize that so many people die by gun violence through homicides, suicides, and unintentional shootings every single day? That children die because adults are irresponsible in keeping their guns locked and stored properly? We have a national problem that affects each and every one of us.

We need commonsense to prevail in Congress! We need universal background checks for every gun purchase. We need reciprocity laws that cover gun laws from state to state. And we need to close the loopholes in our laws. Dylann Roof should not have been able to buy a gun legally. He had confessed to illegal drug possession, and, under South Carolina law, he was not eligible to buy a gun.

Every gun seller has to submit a background check form to the FBI on every buyer. The background check is supposed to be completed within a three-day period. Here's the loophole: If the FBI report doesn't come back within three days, the seller can go ahead and sell the gun to the buyer. Dylann Roof's background check didn't come back in time, so he was able to purchase a gun.

Subsequently, the survivors and the families of the nine people killed at Emanuel are suing the FBI for wrongful deaths, in the hopes that it will force the Department of Justice to close the loopholes in our gun laws. We want to stretch the amount of time for the background check, so people like Dylann Roof can't get their hands on guns.

We also need to ban automatic and semi-automatic weapons. Period. Nobody needs to own an AR15. Those guns are made for hunting humans, and they need to go.

We need to acknowledge the connection between guns and racism. Studies also show that black people disproportionately are being killed by guns. Americans are afraid of black men, and, so, many of our gun laws reflect that fear.

"I need a gun to protect my family." That's the argument. But studies have shown repeatedly that you are much more likely to be killed by your own gun than by an intruder's.

We have let ourselves get duped into forgetting what the Second Amendment was *really* about. We forget about the "well-regulated militia." We just want our guns. And eventually, the very thing we thought was going to protect us will come back to bite us.

When I started speaking out, I thought that I would encounter a lot of haters, but I haven't. I've never been heckled. I know haters are out there, but not where I am, maybe because everybody who comes to hear us speak wants to be there.

A lady came up to me after I gave a talk at Owens Community College in Ohio. "Well, I'm a gun owner…"

It was like she wanted me to engage her. I made a conscious decision: *I'm not gonna try and convince this lady. I'm gonna listen to her, and be as humble as I can.* When she had finished, I responded, "Ma'am, I respect the fact that you are a gun owner. And everybody who wants to own a gun, I believe, should be able to go through a background check. But I just pray that you keep your guns locked up if you have kids."

That was the first time somebody really tried, to my face, to challenge the advocacy work that I'm doing. But other than that, I've never had anybody be mean or hostile or anything.

Usually, people want to hug me, give their condolences, or talk about where they were when they heard about the killings at the church. The more I travel, the more I understand how the deaths of those nine people at Emanuel affected others—and, not just black people. People from all walks of life, no matter their gender or race or religion, have shared heartfelt words of comfort or a warm embrace with me.

One time after an event, a young woman told me she had been sexually abused at home, but her mother had not believed her. She was struggling with how to forgive her abuser. She worried that her faith wasn't strong enough because she couldn't get to forgiveness.

"You don't have to rush that," I told her. "You can take your time and work through that. And if you're not ready to forgive him, then you don't have to. But you also don't have to let him make you feel powerless—because you are not."

Part of the message I bring is that forgiveness doesn't happen overnight, and that's okay. God is always with us, and we are empowered to speak our truth.

I want people of faith to know that you can get over whatever you've been through. Sometimes people treat God like a magic pill— you pray to God and He's supposed to magically fix things. It's not that simple, and all the onus isn't just on God. Christians have work to do; so whatever lane you are in, drive!

As I share my story, I hear other people's stories too. And that's pretty exhausting, because usually by the time I have finished with my presentation, I'm already emotionally drained. But this is my ministry now, because it's Spirit-driven.

I used to wonder: *Did I push myself on people? Or is this really God? Is this my ego, or is this God?* I've always come back to this: I could never have accomplished everything I have done if it wasn't God-driven. I can't just fake my way through. If you put up a façade, it's going to crack after a while, because it isn't real. My ministry is authentic, even though it's sometimes painful and exhausting.

On May 13, 2018, I returned to Emanuel African Methodist Episcopal Church to preach on Mother's Day. I used two scriptures:

> In Him also we have obtained an inheritance, being predestined according to the purpose of Him who works all things according to the counsel of His will. (Ephesians 1:11, NKJV)
>
> It was good for me to be afflicted so that I might learn your decrees. (Psalm 119:71)

The last time I had been in that pulpit was when Rev. Pinkney invited me to preach after Nadine's wedding in 2011. I believe that was the day that Momma truly believed and understood my calling into ministry. And like that day in 2011, I knew that on this Mother's Day she was sitting close by, along with Daddy, Terrie, and Esther.

Here is what I preached that morning:

> "It was good for me to be afflicted so that I might learn your decrees."
>
> On June 17, 2015, the world mourned with us as we had to say goodbye to our family. Evil attempted to find a home in this church. Evil came to seek and destroy, and what it found was nine faithful souls willing to die because God needed them that night.
>
> God had another plan. But to be honest, I didn't see God's plan right away. If I'm gonna be honest, there was a time all I did was scream and holler at God. Even in the midst of my silence, there was screaming. I was praying more than I ever had in my life. I was learning God's decrees again. I had to be reminded who I depended on. I knew God was right there, hovering over me.
>
> I didn't want,...nor thought I had the strength, to deal with all the issues that came from those tragic deaths. Forgiveness, racism, the death penalty—all of a sudden, we were faced with all of this in a very public arena. I couldn't see the divine affliction we all had to bear with their brutal deaths. Yet through all the grief, heartache, and pain, my mother left a legacy—in spite of the storms she had in her life—that I can't ignore.
>
> A legacy is inevitable. We will pass things down to the next generation. Even if we don't have much materially to leave behind, we leave our children and grandchildren with our

faith traditions and beliefs, character traits, talents, hobbies, skills, and family secrets. Family shames, family dysfunctions.

My Grandmother Emily taught Momma how to be resilient, how to cook, how be respectful, how to work hard, how to care about her appearance, how to keep a clean house, on and on; things we don't think about but come naturally. So, as we moved from Grandmother to Momma, her legacy is more than being one of the nine killed in this church. Her legacy is being a faithful believer in Jesus Christ—loyal, resilient, courageous, giving—a go-getter, like so many of you here today.

But how valuable will your legacy be? Will your legacy be one of God and faith, or of the world? Because, we as humans can get caught up in the chaos and afflictions of this world. We can get caught up in drugs, alcohol, domestic violence, mental health issues, cancer, financial situations, sexual abuse—just so much. I can go on and on about the things passed down from generation to generation, the legacy of the "not-so-pretty." It's a legacy we didn't want; a legacy that is embedded in the fabric of our souls. A legacy of secrets and conflicts that were never resolved, and certainly not talked about. These are generational curses, if I can define them as such; the legacy that families don't want to talk about. The legacy of keeping quiet.

We have a God who left us an inheritance, where the afflictions are nothing compared to the joy of knowing that God walks with us and feels our pain, soothes us and comforts us during the time of affiliations.

Matthew 5:10 tells us, "Blessed are those who are persecuted because of righteousness, for theirs is the kingdom of heaven."

My family had to confront issues that were never resolved. Momma, in all her strength and courage, did not like when conflicts and issues arose in the family. She hated confrontations and pressed things down. She would always tell me, "Sharon, be the bigger person. Be the bigger person, Rev. Risher." When I heard those words, I knew it was time to squash that subject.

My family and others' families found themselves dealing with issues that were beyond our control. My family's conscience was gone; the gloves were off and sides were taken. The spiritual wound took an emotional toll on all of us. Things boiled over and over, and are still boiling three years later. Yet, although we have been afflicted with a pain and grief beyond a human understanding, God in God's sovereignty has allowed this pain to move me to a place of total dependence on Him, to learn His decrees over and over again.

I had no choice but to cling to my faith, knowing that, come what may, I had to stand firm in my convictions and beliefs. I had to pray and really do some self-reflection and understand what God said. I had to navigate my way, holding on to God's unchanging hand—kicking and screaming, realizing bit by bit that God is in control. I just had to be open and obedient to know the plan God had for me and you and all of us living and breathing. God needed to awaken us to a struggle that has to be fought again.

The Bible tell us: "If my people, who are called by my name, will humble themselves and pray and seek my face and turn from their wicked ways, then I will hear from heaven, and I will forgive their sin and will heal their land." (2 Chronicles 7:14)

Today, in this season of my life, I refuse to carry those not-so-positive legacy makers with me. I refuse to sit back and not be all I can be through Christ Jesus, who strengthens me. I will carry the afflictions, lessons, and sufferings God has placed upon my life, in order that God's will be done. My path had been laid out for me a long time ago, for such a time as this. People, we are in a war, and the legacy we leave our children and our children's children will follow them the rest of their lives, unless we begin to do something different.

As followers of Christ, we will suffer tribulation, even more than unbelievers, owing to the hostile reaction of the evil world, and similar to that which afflicted Christ Himself. In this life, we will suffer, we will be broken, we will walk through the valley of death, yet God walks right alongside us. God promises us in Isaiah 40:31, "but those who hope in the LORD / will renew their strength. / They will soar on wings like eagles; / they will run and not grow weary, / they will walk and not be faint."

My mother left me a platform for invoking change and a means for addressing racism, working toward forgiveness, and addressing gun violence—which is perpetuated mostly against people of color. I'm humbled and grateful to travel across this country telling the story of what happened in this church. I have been places I'd never imagined going, and met people I would never have thought about meeting. The divine affliction placed upon me is producing the outcomes God designed it do.

Activism is hard work: it's not always wins; sometimes there are losses.

Many times since I started volunteering with the Everytown Survivor Network and Moms Demand Action I have wanted to quit. Ending gun violence, while an enormously popular idea, is excruciatingly difficult work. Even though the majority of Americans want commonsense gun laws, a startlingly low number of people are willing to do the work to make it happen. They are busy, or they are afraid to speak up or take action, or they believe they can't have an impact. I used to be one of those people. But innocent people kept getting killed. The number of preventable deaths continued to grow. There have been so many deaths, accidental and intentional—so often, everywhere—that I actually began to fear for my own children. That fear drives me.

The most valuable legacy we can pass to our children is a spiritual legacy of faith in Christ. Momma left that most important legacy to me—that, no matter what, God will provide; that, if you work hard, stay humble, and talk to God, God will be there when no one else is.

Although every individual must make a personal decision for Christ, there are things we can do to create an atmosphere where faith can thrive. When we consistently show our children the value and relevancy of faith in Christ, that's a legacy not easily tossed aside.

God knew the necessity of one generation passing the torch of faith to the next. He even laid out a plan for us in His Word. When Israel was poised to enter the Promised Land, God—through Moses—told the people how vital it would be not only to model faith to their children but also to purposefully teach them God's Word. Knowing and obeying God would keep them right in the center of His will and blessing.

A legacy is not a resume or list of accomplishments. A legacy is the imprint you leave on the future. As a result, we all have a legacy, and we will leave it either by default or design. We all are legacy makers.

No matter what lane you find yourself in, you have a job to be all God created you to be, because you are a child of the Highest God!

I challenge each one of you here today to make a conscious decision to think about what your legacy will be. We have a choice about how we are gonna live this life God has allowed us to have, to make use of the second and third and fourth chances God has given us.

God has commanded us to come under Him and learn his decrees. Write them on your hearts and watch how your legacy will produce great followers of Christ. To God be all the glory!

I didn't go downstairs to the fellowship hall for dinner after I preached on Mother's Day, because that's where the killings happened. I just didn't feel like going down there. I have been downstairs only once or twice since Momma died.

I have happy memories of that room from before the shootings. I remember eating breakfast down there before church, while Momma worked the meal. And later, when I would come home from college, having breakfast downstairs was something I always knew I was gonna do with Momma. Back then she would make us go to the seven o'clock morning service. I'd come home from college and hang out with my friends on Saturday night. But Momma would just be looking at you like, "I don't care what time you get home; just know that you *are* getting up for church."

They placed a cross in that section where they were killed, with the names of the people who died. The few times I've gone down there since, I've felt compelled to run my hand over the names.

But most times I just can't go down there. Once, Esther and I participated in a Showtime documentary on the Charleston shootings. While we were filming our segment, they wanted me to go down there—and they were really depending on that little piece—but I just could not do it. And I didn't do it.

It's really almost the same thing for me with the church—the whole building. Some days it's very overwhelming and I get really choked up. And then on other days it's okay, because there's a good spirit there. It doesn't ever feel like a haunted place. I just feel sad that she's not there.

When I go there, I still feel the power and the magnificence and the presence of all of the saints that came before in that church. I can still see Momma in that church. Regardless of when I go, I can see my momma in different places at that church. Like, I can see her downstairs with the vacuum cleaner, or upstairs working in the sanctuary.

Before the shooting, Gary and Esther sometimes would go to the church and help Momma. Momma had two knee replacements so she would give them some gas money or whatever to come to the church and help her vacuum. Gary would help her strip the floors downstairs.

My momma did all that stuff—stripping, cleaning, and shining the floors. That had been a part of her duties with the Gaillard Center maintenance crew.

Afterward, whenever I did go into the downstairs bathroom, I was like, *Mm-hmm. They don't keep it clean like Mama did. Nobody gets it clean like Mama. She'd have it smellin' all good.*

Momma would take her own money and buy air fresheners and things. She also bought paint and painted both the women's and the men's restrooms. That's who she was. She always wanted things to be nice and smelling good.

CHAPTER 9

Another Funeral

In 2015, after Momma died, Esther visited me in Dallas, and I was shocked at how thin she'd become. Esther had always been chunky, so her size nearly bowled me over. I didn't ask if anything was wrong. Maybe I should have, but I felt like she would have said something if she wanted to talk about it. I didn't want to pry.

Looking back, I think she was already pretty sick, but she never said. Esther died on November 4, 2017. It was a blow out of the blue.

I still think about the last time I spoke to Esther. I had a hard "come to Jesus" talk with her. I had been helping Esther financially for a while. After the shootings at the church, a lot of people had donated money to the families, and the church dispersed the funds. Everybody got a nice little piece of money. But when people have never had money, often they don't know what to do with it when they get some. Neither Esther nor Gary knew how to manage money, so they quickly went through all that they got.

Esther never came right out and told me her money was gone. She just started asking me for help with this bill and that bill. Finally, I just came out and asked, "Esther, you don't have no damn money, do you?"

She started to cry. "I didn't want you to be ashamed of me."

I helped her out as best as I could. *That's my sister, and this money came because our Momma died. I'm not gonna sit here and not take care of my sister.*

I was proud I could help, because there was a time when it was really hard for me financially. In Dallas, though, I was still on a limited budget. Esther would call me for help, and I would scrimp together what I could and send her money.

Eventually, I just started getting the account numbers for her water bill or light bill or whatever and pay them directly. I felt the responsibility of being the oldest, even though her poor money management got on my nerves.

Esther had always made bad financial decisions. She would give people money to help them pay their damned light bill, and then hers would be cut off. I never could understand that. She gave money to JonQuil and a lot of other people. She bought some new furniture for her house she didn't really need. Sometimes, she would rent a car.

So that day I had fussed at her because I had gotten tired of trying to take care of her and me. "Esther, you've gotta get a job. You gotta do something, because I can't afford to keep you and me both up." I was kind of hard on her.

"Yeah, Sharon, I know... I know, Sharon, I know I gotta do better... I gotta do better."

That was on Thursday. The next day, I didn't hear from her, which was hard, because we talked *every* day.

Saturday morning came, and I still hadn't heard from her. *Boy, is she mad at me. Well, I don't care, I'm gonna call her, anyway. Let me just call my sister to check on her.*

I didn't get an answer. I called again, and no answer.

Later that morning, I laid down to take a nap. My phone kept ringing while I was asleep. *I'll get it later.* When I woke up, I saw all the missed calls.

I called Esther's number again. Her neighbor's daughter answered, "Miss Sharon, I'm so sorry. Esther is dead."

People had seen her outside that morning. Esther knew how to be a good neighbor. She would open her front door and people would know that she was up. She often sat on the little stoop that was her front porch. People had seen her sitting out there and said hello to her that morning.

I guess she went back into the house and couldn't catch her breath. She had chronic obstructive pulmonary disease, COPD. We knew that, but she never really talked about it. We always had to pry things out of her. She didn't have an oxygen tank; just her inhaler. Sometimes she would have a coughing fit, but it never lasted very long. I guess we never knew how bad her COPD was.

That morning, someone went to check on Esther and found her on the floor with her asthma pump in her hand. The doctors said she died of acute respiratory failure.

I believe that when I was trying to call Esther, she was in her house dying or had already died.

Truthfully, Esther never really recovered from Momma's death. She would call me crying and upset. I would listen and use soothing words to calm her down. Sometimes we cried together. She would talk about being hurt at "the sisters" being torn apart, about how she got sick during Momma's funeral and missed most of the service, about how much she missed Momma. She would just cry and cry.

I regretted my last words to Esther. *I shouldn't have fussed at her. Maybe I could have helped her. What am I gonna do now? I don't have nobody.*

On Monday I drove to Charleston and stayed at Esther's house while we planned the funeral. I knew that I couldn't afford to stay in a hotel because of what was gonna have to happen financially. In my heart I already knew Esther didn't have life insurance.

It was strange to be in Esther's house without her being there. The neighbors came by in streams. People kept talking about how nice Esther was, how kind, and how funny. Everybody loved Esther.

I never had to worry about food or cooking while I was there. Her friends, especially Miss Abby, cooked and brought food almost every night. They had cleaned the house before I arrived, so it was nice and neat and smelling good.

Miss Abby is like those neighborhood women where we grew up. You could always depend on Miss Abby to help you out. She was a fabulous cook too. So the whole time I was there, Miss Abby made sure there was food for people coming in and out. She knew Esther loved crabs, so one night they had just a big crab boil. They fried fish and cooked crabs and all of the fixings. Everybody just ate. *This is for you, Esther.*

It was nice to see that Esther had such good friends. She deserved them, because Esther had a hard life. She was the sibling who never quite got a sure footing in life. She was always a bit slow in school, but she tried really hard. I think she got "socially promoted" along the way.

But if you got into trouble, you wanted Esther on your side. She was the ride or die sister. If something was going on in your life and you needed backup, you called Esther. All you had to say was, "Esther, I need you," and she was on her way.

Growing up, if Nadine got into a disagreement with somebody, she would run to Esther, who was older and kind of like the family enforcer. Esther loved a fight, and since she was always kind of chunky growing up, if something went down, you called her. She was going to handle it! She didn't get into much trouble herself, though, because everybody loved Esther.

She played baseball on the parks and recreation teams, and when she got a hold of that ball, she hit it and it was gone! Her jersey number was nine, and everybody started calling her Big Nine.

Esther and Nadine had gotten really close after Terrie and I left for college. They were even roommates for a while. They got pregnant at about the same time and lived together while they were expecting. Because they stayed in Charleston, they got really, really close through the years.

Esther didn't go to college. She held a lot of different jobs, but the one she held the longest was at a dry cleaner. Esther knew how to make clothes look good. Momma taught all of us to iron, but Esther *really* knew how to iron clothes. And because she worked at the cleaner's, Momma and everybody else would take their clothes there.

After Momma died, I was speaking at a church in Charleston, and my robe needed to be ironed. I started ironing the robe and Esther said, "Girl, move out the way. You don't know what you're doing. Give me that thing. You can't go outta here all wrinkled up in that thing. Momma would have a fit!"

She got a hold of that robe with her regular old ironing board, an iron, and a spray bottle, and she did that robe up. It was beautiful!

Esther gave birth to JonQuil when she was in her early thirties and raised him as a single parent. She struggled a lot to pay bills on time and make enough money. She did all right when it was just her, but it got a lot harder after she had a child.

For a while, she worked at a nursing home in the kitchen, serving on the line. And she would have to take meals to the patients' rooms. One time when I was home, I went with her while she delivered food trays. Everybody just loved her. No one would have ever thought that she struggled to maintain a decent home for her and JonQuil. She was so cheerful and so funny.

Eventually she got Section 8 housing, which gave them a decent place to live. She also got JonQuil a Big Brother through that organization. She always did her best to make sure JonQuil had the things he needed. She would always call Momma if something fell short. Momma would fuss, but she would always help Esther out.

Momma was there for all of us. She would fuss, but she would do her best for all her children.

Momma babysat a lot because my sisters had their babies just a few months apart. Esther had JonQuil in June. Terrie's daughter, Najee, and Nadine's daughter, Nadhina, were born in October of the same year. In fact, Nadhina and Najee were born an hour apart in the same hospital. Their rooms were right next door to each other. Momma said the nurses were laughing at her as she went from one room to the next. "Miss Lance, you need roller skates!"

After Terrie went on disability, she took care of all three kids at Momma's house until people got off work. Lord, she was a hard taskmaster! Terrie would make them do their homework as soon as they got home, and then check it to make sure they kept up with everything.

JonQuil was a good student through elementary school and into high school. He and his mother lived in Mount Pleasant, which is across the bridge from Charleston.

But something happened to JonQuil when he was at Wando High School that really changed things for him. Esther told me that JonQuil was on the football team and somebody said something very hurtful and very racial to him. Wando was predominantly white. From that point on, Esther said JonQuil didn't want to be in school. He didn't even want to play football.

JonQuil and Esther were really close. It was just the two of them, after all. She was so proud that JonQuil made good grades and that he'd talked about going to college. But whatever happened when he was in the tenth grade hurt him deeply, and eventually he dropped out of school.

I got really mad at Esther for letting him drop out, because I knew the odds of him returning to school were low. He was now in the high-risk category for young black males in his age range.

To his credit, JonQuil has managed to avoid many of the pitfalls that trap young black men. He's is a hard worker. Charleston has more restaurants and hotels than you can believe, so he keeps a job. His main motivation now is his son—JonQuil Devin Lance Jr. Everybody calls him Junior.

That baby was Esther's pride and joy. She loved that baby! I keep in touch with him and his daddy. I call and help him out when I can to make sure Junior gets presents at Christmas and birthdays. Esther would be glad that I keep up with them.

* * * * *

Growing up, Esther and I had always been close; but when I went to college, that closeness diminished a bit. Even after I got out of college and would come home to visit, we always got together. Still, we weren't as close as we had been.

Then, after Momma died, we got as close as two sisters can be.

One time after Momma died I came to visit Esther. Her friends told me how Esther had painted the house and cleaned up and everything. She was telling everybody, "My sister is coming to stay with *me!*"

It was important to her because nobody ever stayed at Esther's house. Esther lived in North Charleston, where there is a lot of crime and gun violence. I made up my mind to face it, even though I was kind of scared of the neighborhood. *This is my sister. I'm not gonna make her feel bad. I'm gonna go there and I'm gonna stay at her house and spend time with her.*

Her friends talked about how proud she was. She wanted everyone to know, "My big sister is coming. My big sister is coming." And she wanted everything to look good when I arrived.

As scary as that neighborhood was, Esther was not afraid. She had eked out her own little space. Nobody bothered her because everybody there knew her, and they all loved her.

One time I was visiting her, and she said, "Let's walk to the store." There was a little corner store maybe half a block from her house.

I said, "Well, Esther, you got to lock everything up."

"Girl, no. We ain't gotta lock nothing up. Come on."

We walked to the store and back. No one bothered her. No one bothered her house.

And all along the walk people were calling out to her. "Hey, Esther! What's up?" Everyone knew her.

Esther and I were featured in an episode of Showtime's documentary series *Active Shooter.* The series has episodes on a lot of the mass shootings in the United States, including those at the Aurora, Colorado, movie theater and the Pulse Nightclub in Orlando. The third episode was about the shootings at Emanuel. Esther and I were the only ones from our family who participated. Esther really didn't want to at first, but I convinced her to do it.

They filmed us just being together and cooking Momma's favorite meal. I'm glad that I'll always have that episode on DVD to remember my time with Esther. I'm going to make a copy for JonQuil so that someday Junior will be able to see his grandmother.

I'm also grateful that she flew to visit me in Dallas, and that she went with us to that White House Christmas party. Because of what happened to Momma, Esther did get to travel a little bit and see some things. She even traveled to Austin, Texas, to hear me preach at my alma mater, Austin Presbyterian Theological Seminary. I was the guest preacher for the annual Martin Luther King Jr. celebration at the seminary. Esther was so happy to be there, especially since she hadn't been able to make the trip for my graduation.

The seminary also honored Momma in a very special way. Just outside the front chapel transept is the Ethel Lance Memorial, a space for spiritual reflection with benches and a marker dedicated to Momma. The seminary also established the Ethel W. Lance Human and Civil Rights Award. It was established with a gift from First Presbyterian Church in Cuero, Texas, in Momma's memory. The award is given annually to a graduating senior who has demonstrated outstanding contributions to human or civil rights while enrolled at the seminary.

* * * * *

In Charleston, just before the trial of Momma's killer started in November 2016, Emanuel opened the Empowerment Center to offer support, counseling, and help for the survivors and family members of victims. Esther got very involved with the center.

Miss Tenelle Jones, the outreach therapist for the Empowerment Center, really took to Esther, and my sister felt really, really comfortable with her. At first Miss Tenelle started coming to Esther's house for sessions, because Esther didn't have a car and she couldn't get downtown. Eventually Miss Tenelle talked her into coming to the church for grief support group sessions on Thursdays. Afterward, Esther would call me and say, "Girl, we had a good talk today at the Empowerment Center." She loved going there. She even went on a couple of victim awareness retreats.

Esther had a saying whenever things got rough or funny or whatever: "Hold my hand, Pastor. Hold my hand." So the people at the Empowerment Center called her "Hold My Hand, Pastor."

Esther always had a joke. She would make everybody laugh, and it made their time go by because she made it light. Even though the group would be talking about heavy things, she would always find a way to make them laugh. After Esther's funeral, people from the Empowerment Center talked about how they were going to miss their "Hold My Hand, Pastor."

* * * * *

When it was time to for plan my sister's funeral, it just seemed like too much loss for one family. Plus I had no idea how we were going to pay for it. Once I got into Charleston, I called Nadine again and I left a message. "If you want to help plan our sister's funeral, I will be at the funeral home at [this time on this day]."

I didn't know whether she was gonna show, but she did. JonQuil, Nadine, Aja, and I sat together at the funeral home to plan Esther's service. The expenses totaled about fourteen thousand dollars.

Lord, how we gonna pay for this? We had looked for insurance policies, but we knew there wasn't one. I thought for a bit about getting her cremated because that would be cheaper, but JonQuil was against it. "No, I don't want my momma cremated," he said, so I went along with that.

Maybe things could have been cheaper, but I did not want my sister to be buried cheaply. I stuck my neck out and signed those papers, then I begged for money to bury her.

I reached out to Rev. Eric Manning at Emanuel. "Rev. Manning, we don't have any money to bury her. You know, I've got a little bit of money that I can put in, but it won't go far."

He said, "Sharon, don't you worry about it. Cause we gonna send her off nice."

The church did their part, and a group from the chaplains' association that had been involved with the families during the trial made a donation of three thousand dollars. I even started a GoFundMe page on Facebook, and the response was very good. I must have given about three or four thousand dollars myself. I'm still paying on the funeral—one hundred and fifty dollars every month.

Rev. Manning really did make sure that everything was nice for her. Miss Abby, Esther's longtime friend and neighbor, asked if she could buy my sister's outfit for being laid out in the coffin.

"Thank you so much," I told her. "I would appreciate that if you did."

Esther's funeral was not like Momma's. I made sure it was a nice, very personal, and very tasteful service. And I made sure it was at Mother Emanuel.

Rev. Manning delivered the eulogy. My ex-husband played "Amazing Grace" on the saxophone, and it was beautiful. Esther and Bernard always got along. Even after we divorced, she continued to call him her brother-in-law. "We are brother-in-law and sister-in-law till the day we die," she'd say.

Nobody had wanted Bernard to play at Terrie's service, even though we had reconciled. And it really would have been a war if I had asked Bernard to play for Momma's service, so I left that alone. But nobody was gonna tell me what to do with Esther's service.

Since Esther was such a jovial person, I wanted some upbeat music. JonQuil and I spoke. Esther herself looked beautiful, and the service was beautiful. She had a real good crowd. Her flowers were beautiful. The folks from Esther's neighborhood showed up in force, including Miss Abby and her girls. Gary and his family were there, and so were Nadine and her husband and daughter. Terrie's daughter, Najee, came too. A lot of people from the Empowerment Center and the church were there.

We did not want the repast in the church's Fellowship Hall, so the church secured the school across the street, the school I attended as a child. It's a charter school now, and people would give their eye teeth to have their children go there.

The church had the food catered at their expense—chicken, green beans, corn, desserts, and all that kind of stuff. It was really nice. A lot of people came, and I walked around and thanked people for coming.

Nadine was crying and hugging everybody. She hugged my daughter. *Oh my Lord, the church is getting ready to blow the hell up!* She hugged Bernard. She talked with JonQuil at the repast. She talked with me for a little while. But after the repast, we went back to our corners.

I have not seen Nadine since that day.

We buried Esther very close to where Momma and Terrie are laid to rest. It just so happened that a nearby plot was available at the cemetery. God worked that out for Esther to lie near them.

There wasn't much to Esther's estate. Lord knows, she didn't have a lot. I took a sweater, a jacket, and a pillow off of her bed. JonQuil gave me a painting she had done in one of her therapy groups at the Empowerment Center. Just things that make me feel close to her. I have the eyeglasses that she used to wear…little things.

I headed back to Charlotte right after the funeral, as I had to hit the road for a speaking engagement a week or so afterward. That was *hard*. I really got emotional during the speech and had to confess to the audience, "Please bear with me, I just buried my sister."

Losing Esther really made me feel like I had no more family. True, I have my kids, but it still felt like all my family was gone. I miss Momma. I miss Esther. I miss Terrie. And I miss Nadine.

CHAPTER 10

Talking Race

I am a proud daughter of the American South, a true Geechie girl from the Low Country of South Carolina and a product of the civil rights era. My Southern black heritage has shaped me into the woman of faith I am today. But like many African Americans from the South, I am no stranger to the hate and intolerance that has defined a large part of our history. I still see it on a daily basis.

I don't know if I had buried my head in the sand, but before the death of those nine souls in Charleston, I didn't realize how many people subscribed to a white supremacist/white nationalist ideology. I understand the reality of racism and prejudice, but I wanted to believe that the level of racial hatred that drives people to kill was in the past. It's definitely not.

Again and again, blood is shed in this country because of racism. On Saturday, August 12, 2017, in Charlottesville, Virginia, a speeding car rammed into anti-racist protesters, killing young Heather Heyer and injuring at least nineteen others. The country witnessed the death of an innocent woman—again—because of white supremacist ideology and hate. That really got to me.

In October 2018, another damned killing by a white supremacist, this time in Jeffersontown, Kentucky. A middle-aged white man killed Maurice E. Stallard in a Kroger store and Vickie Lee Jones on the parking lot. Both victims were black, and the shooter reportedly commented to a white person on the parking lot, "whites don't shoot whites." Earlier, the shooter had tried to get into a church whose black congregants were gathered for a midweek service, but he couldn't get in the locked doors.

So because of these and other blatant acts of hate, I became what some people may call an accidental activist. An accidental activist is someone who is thrust into a life-altering experience and then springs into action for specific causes or issues. Not every activist starts out with the goal of affecting great change in the wider world. Most begin by bringing change to wherever they are. Some of our lives are shaped by chance, quirks of timing, and strange coincidences. Our unwillingness or simple inability to ignore social injustice propels us to action.

So from the outside it looks like I entered this arena by accident. But on a spiritual level, I know that this little ol' Geechie girl was chosen a long time ago for such a time as this. All the struggles, challenges, and obstacles in my life, and in my mother's life, have placed me where I am today. That moment when Momma called me to come and hear Dr. Martin Luther King Jr. speak those many years ago helped set the stage for me to be an advocate today.

When Dr. King was young, inexperienced in matters of public leadership, he was called to give direction to a march for freedom the likes of which human history had never known. The ink was still wet on his terminal theological degree, but he was the chosen one. He advocated nonviolence, yet his life, and the lives of all who marched with him, faced threats of violence every day.

On Sunday, March 31, 1968, Dr. King preached his final sermon at Washington National Cathedral. From that massive pulpit, he delivered a sermon titled, "Remaining Awake Through a Great Revolution." Dr. King was speaking prophetically when he said, "It is no longer a choice, my friends, between violence and nonviolence. It is either nonviolence or nonexistence."

King was adamant that Americans—not just black people, but all people—not sleep through the great revolution we are (still) witnessing. We must stay awake and commit ourselves to enter on the side of God's love and justice.

Racism did not die because of the civil rights movement. Racism did not go away when Barack Obama was elected President. Racism is an infection that continues to fester in this country.

Having a black President scared a lot of white losers. "Oh, we can't have that, because now they'll want to take over." America is not going to let *that* happen. Sometimes I wonder if we will ever have another black President. If we ever have a woman President—damn it, I sure would like her to be black!

The political environment today proves that racism didn't disappear after a black President was elected. Scratch the surface and it's there. Society has tried to make it appear that, since blacks have made strides, there's no need for more conversations about race. We have achieved a lot of things, but America's deep-seated racism still has life.

The current administration has unleashed an atmosphere in which people feel, "I don't have to hide that no more. I'm gonna just be who I am. I don't like black people, Muslims, Jews...whoever. I don't have to hide behind trying to be a good soul. I can just say and do what I want, because the President does. And because, damn it, we run this country, and we are always gonna keep power."

We say we want a country that gives all an opportunity to share in its bounty. If Americans truly want what we say—if we want this country to live out the true meaning of its creed—then we have to get real about how deeply racism is rooted in this foundation. Everybody is worthy of a share. There's enough for everybody!

Some people say they get tired of talking about race. We have to talk about race and racism in the United States. Conversations about racism in this country must never stop, even when they're hard—especially when they're hard. If you're not willing to be moved out of your comfortable space, you aren't going to change. You have to be uncomfortable. If you're white, you're gonna have to acknowledge that the color of your skin brings privilege in this country that is not afforded to people of color.

I just wish America would just acknowledge its racist past, and the disgrace of slavery and hatred. The disgrace of enslaving an entire race. The disgrace of nearly wiping out the Native American population. Our country has done things that were thoroughly wrong.

America didn't just hurt black people. Our nation has hurt every indigenous group it has encountered. America brought the slaves here. Black people learned everything that America did not want us to learn. And because we're trying to do the same thing white people are doing—trying to have the American dream like everybody else—some people are mad at that. They still want to be in control. They still want to keep us down, even though everything we know we assimilated from them!

In the late 1960s, a collection of musicians and artists performed spoken word under the name The Last Poets. They were kind of like the early rappers, and they were all about black empowerment. One thing they said has stuck in my mind. And I hate to admit this, but it sums up what I truly believe: "The white man has a God complex." So to many white people, they're gods. And that crazy understanding gives them the motivation to say, "I'm superior. And I'm always gonna be superior."

I feel that is specifically the case in North America because of slavery. And this is what we must fight against every damned day in America.

Someone asked me one time how it is that I don't hate all white people. I laughed and said, "You gotta dig real deep."

It's tempting sometimes to give in to the anger. But you have to have the spirit of the Holy Ghost inside of you. You can't just group everybody in the same category. You can't lump everybody into one big pot hole, because that's what society has done with black people.

Society views us all the same. There are ascriptions for black people—no matter how well we have done, no matter how educated we are, how successful—we're still just black. Since Now that I've reached age 60, I've learned that you have to judge each person individually. Then, too, you've got to be careful about judging people at all, because we all are flawed, regardless of color. Some of the best people in my life are not black.

Each of us has an opportunity to have a voice in this democracy through our privilege and sacred right to vote. We all have something to contribute to this world to make it better.

It's our duty, especially African Americans. So many of our people were threatened, beaten, or killed so that we could obtain the right to vote. It's important to go to the polls and vote in local elections. Vote in state elections. Vote in national elections. Vote for candidates who promote equality and decency. Vote for candidates who will stand up to the gun lobbyists and work toward sensible gun laws.

Racism, poverty, and gun violence are intertwined. Everytown has a lot of information available on its website about guns and race, including these two facts:

- "Gun homicides are concentrated in cities—half of all gun homicides took place in just 127 cities, which represent nearly a quarter of the U.S. population. Within these cities, gun homicides are most prevalent in racially segregated neighborhoods with high rates of poverty."[1]
- "Black Americans represent the majority of gun homicide victims. In fact, Black Americans are ten times more likely than white Americans to die by gun homicide."[2]

---

[1] Everytown.org citing Aliza Aufrichtig, Lois Beckett, Jan Diehm, and Jamiles Lartey, "Want to Fix Gun Violence in America? Go Local," theguardian.com, https://www.theguardian.com/us-news/ng-interactive/2017/jan/09/special-report-fixing-gun-violence-in-america.

[2] Everytown.org citing Centers for Disease Control and Prevention study, "WONDER, Underlying Cause of Death," a five-year (2013–2017) average of gun deaths by race.

In a CNN.com article on April 24, 2018, journalist Jacqueline Howard wrote about a study on the disparities between how black and white men die by gun violence:

"Compared with white men, the researchers found that black men experienced 27 more firearm homicides per 100,000 people annually nationwide (29.12 for black men vs. 2.1 for white men). The states with the highest rates of firearm homicide among black men in the data— namely, Missouri, Michigan, Illinois, and Indiana—also had the largest disparities between blacks and whites, the researchers found."[3]

Lately I have been asked over and over, "Have you thought about running for political office?" The question surprised me the first time, so I answered something like: "Let's see what God says about that."

The funny thing is, when I was younger, going into politics was my game plan. Way back when, I really thought I knew what I wanted to do with my life: I was going to go to college, then law school, and then move into politics. I had in my head that I would speak for those who couldn't speak for themselves. I even dreamed of being the first black lady mayor of Charleston. But life happened and not all of those dreams came to pass. I did accomplish a lot, though, and I'm good with that. (By the way, a black woman still hasn't become mayor of Charleston yet, so that is still to happen—just maybe not for me.)

The route I took was not the way I had planned, but politics is my ministry now. I'm a politician in the army of God. My weaponry is love—sharing the good news of Jesus Christ. I make people uncomfortable with the raw truth and then make them listen to the things they need to hear from someone like me. If you're willing to hear me and others who will talk to you about race, and who will also listen to you—and, then if you're willing to do one thing, two things you've never done in your life, that's the start. That's how we start to end racism. If everybody's trying to do that, then maybe there will be movement toward us being able to live together peacefully.

Eliminating racism is one of those things for which we're not going to see a major outcome right away. The outcome will manifest as racism and hatred are chipped away, little by little. We have to stay relentless in our pursuit of racial harmony. I know that some people will never move past their hatred and their bigotry. But whatever group of people I'm in front of, I hope that I am able to give them a sense of hope, because there really is hope.

---

3 Jacqueline Howard, "The disparities in how black and white men die in gun violence, state by state," April 24, 2018, cnn.com, https://www.cnn.com/2018/04/23/health/gun-deaths-in-men-by-state-study/index.html .

Let's just start talking! We need honest conversations about race, privilege, and oppression. The more we get together in small groups, the more we can start to understand each other in a real way.

We all are human, and we all have hearts. If we let the Holy Spirit in, then somehow goodness and right will seep into those hearts.

CHAPTER 11

Where Is the Church?

This is how we know what love is: Jesus Christ laid down his life for us. And we ought to lay down our lives for our brothers and sisters. If anyone has material possessions and sees a brother or sister in need but has no pity on them, how can the love of God be in that person? Dear children, let us not love with words or speech but with actions and in truth.

This is how we know that we belong to the truth and how we set our hearts at rest in his presence: If our hearts condemn us, we know that God is greater than our hearts, and he knows everything. Dear friends, if our hearts do not condemn us, we have confidence before God and receive from him anything we ask, because we keep his commands and do what pleases him. And this is his command: to believe in the name of his Son, Jesus Christ, and to love one another as he commanded us. The one who keeps God's commands lives in him, and he in them. And this is how we know that he lives in us: We know it by the Spirit he gave us.

1 John 3:16–24

Sunday after Sunday, we sit in the pews and hear what we believe to be the messages of God, through the authority of Scripture. Sunday after Sunday these sermons are heard, yet hearts stay trapped in old ways of feeling, old ways of thinking, and old ways of believing.

We pick and choose what we will incorporate into our belief system—the issues we will support. We stay in our own little bubble, believing we are good Christians. We feel safe in our beliefs, we feel safe in our church and communities, as their beliefs generally reflect our own.

My mother felt safe in her church. She was murdered there for the color of her skin.

People say, "I'm not a racist." And they believe that. But so many people—well-meaning, church-going people who would never be blatantly hateful or racist—stay silent in the face of racism. They think that because they live in nice, predominantly white, safe communities, they are unaffected by racism. They think, because they have enough to live on, they are unaffected by poverty. They think they will never be affected by a mass shooting where they live.

And I get that. It's easy to stay in our safe little bubbles. Why should we intentionally position ourselves to be uncomfortable? Well friends, here's why: Jesus had to die in order that all humanity be given a chance to live out its faith without any payback.

Being true followers of Christ means that we are sacrificial people. It means believing and doings things that are beyond human understanding. God knew humans needed help and sent His only begotten son to save us. Jesus willingly died on that cross to save us. That is our example of being sacrificial.

So Christians *cannot* be silent on social injustice,—not in these days when social media highlights rampant white supremacy, political chaos, gun violence, immigration issues, nuclear weapons, and on and on; not in these days when social justice seems to be for the other and not for us.

You cannot have social justice without the Gospel. You can accomplish a myriad of good works, subconsciously seeking praise rather than true justice. You can be a genuinely empathetic person and do good things for people while completely ignoring the sovereignty of God. But you cannot have social justice without the Gospel, and you cannot have the Gospel without social justice. You cannot go on mission trips to Africa and Haiti and make excuses for white supremacists in America. You cannot have the Gospel without loving your neighbor as yourself (an explicit commandment given in Matthew 22:39), regardless of race, sexual orientation, socioeconomic status, or gender.

If your Christianity is only for middle-class white people, or people who behave or believe exactly as you do, you have ignored what Jesus called the second greatest commandment. If you donate canned goods and coats at Christmas but stay away from the "bad side of town" the other 364 days of the year, you've ignored that commandment. If you turn a blind eye to racism, you've ignored that commandment.

I've been on mission trips. (I don't think they're a bad thing or a waste of time the way progressives sometimes complain.) But we could make assertions about teenagers who go on mission trips but don't associate with the "rough" kids at their very own high school. We could draw conclusions about people who donate to mission trips but vote for a border wall and a Muslim ban. We could say a lot of things here, but I guess you catch my drift.

We live in a time when, for too many, it appears that loving our brothers and sisters in the manner outlined in Scripture has been forgotten. We carry on with our lives, while all around us, it appears the world is going to hell in a handbasket.

As Christians, we are called to do so much more. As Christians, we must engage the world we live in. We must minister to the poor. We must welcome the stranger. We must reach out to our neighbors— at home, and around the world. And we must address gun violence. Because, when God said, "Thou shall not kill," God meant that!

"Lord, I Want to Be a Christian" is an African American spiritual. It was likely composed in the 1750s by enslaved African American in Virginia who were exposed to the teachings of evangelist Samuel Davies, a Presbyterian minister who preached to and taught the enslaved.

I believe this song captures the essence of what Scripture is telling us today. The love of brother and sister must come from deep within our hearts. God is in the heart of a professed Christian—and, God is love.

I believe that, as people of faith and messengers of God's Word, we have a duty to initiate conversations about race and how congregations can truly understand our call to be with community.

Churches can no longer sit on the sidelines while our sisters and brothers are in need. Dr. King understood that the church has to step up. If our sisters and brothers are hurting, no matter where they are in the world, we hurt also. The church universal must not stay quiet.

> The King will reply, "Truly I tell you, whatever you did for one of the least of these brothers and sisters of mine, you did for me."
>
> Then he will say to those on his left, "Depart from me, you who are cursed, into the eternal fire prepared for the devil and his angels. For I was hungry and you gave me nothing to eat, I was thirsty and you gave me nothing to drink, I was a stranger and you did not invite me in, I needed clothes and you did not clothe me, I was sick and in prison and you did not look after me."

They also will answer, "Lord, when did we see you hungry or thirsty or a stranger or needing clothes or sick or in prison, and did not help you?"

He will reply, "Truly I tell you, whatever you did not do for one of the least of these, you did not do for me."

Matthew 25:40–45

On June 17, 2015, when evil walked into Emanuel AME Church and killed nine people, my life turned upside down. My brain couldn't comprehend how the killer could sit in an hour-long Bible study, hold hands with them, and then pull out a gun and slaughter them. This young white supremacist was convinced that black people were a threat to his way of life. He chose the most sacred of spaces to carry out his vile deed.

As Americans and as citizens of this country, we continue to address racism and gun violence only cosmetically. Our churches continue to struggle in understanding the major role they have to play in reconciliation and hope for all people.

Bishop George Vance Murry, a black Jesuit whose background is in education, summarized Catholic teaching on racism and inequality, noting that the church's teaching on the fundamental dignity of all people has not always been reflected in its actions.

In a lecture at St. Peter's Catholic Church in Charlotte, Bishop Murry said, "American Catholics have shown a lack of moral consciousness on the issue of race... If we are to be true to the principles on which our country was founded and the principles on which our faith is based, we must do much more."

Bishop Murry criticized the church's lethargic response to racism in America, even in the years since the U.S. bishops issued "Brothers and Sisters to Us," a pastoral letter on racism crafted in 1979. That letter called on the Catholic Church to address racism within the church and in the United States. In his talk at St. Peter's, Bishop Murry reminded the church that racism is still alive and well in Catholicism and in our society. He called for more action, more attention, more work to be done to conquer this deeply rooted problem.

"When considering the history of racism in the Catholic Church, one cannot help but wonder why, in the United States, there was so little social consciousness among Catholics regarding racism," Bishop Murry said. "Why does it appear the church in America is incapable of taking decisive action and incapable of enunciating clear-cut principles regarding racism that have led to a change of attitude?

"Racism is a sin that divides the human family and violates the fundamental human dignity of those called to be children of the same Father," he continued, adding that the church must become "a consistent voice" to eradicate it. "If not, we are destined for history to continue to repeat itself, and once again the church will be perceived as a silent observer in the face of racism."[1]

We have placed church dogma before our moral duty to follow the teachings of Jesus Christ. Where are the risk takers in the church? Who among us will preach the sermon that will make their congregation uncomfortable? Who will lead the Bible studies, Sunday school classes, or small group discussions that address the issues of racism and gun violence in America?

Jesus' life provides the model by which we are to work for justice and peace. Like the Old Testament prophets, we must raise our voices for the voiceless and help victims defend themselves from injustice. The church is *commanded* to be the place of refuge. And the people who sit in the pews are the same people who hold the power to be more than donors or churchgoers. They have the power and the potential to be true followers of Christ, true social justice warriors, true rabble-rousers in the name of God! We just have to teach them how to do it.

At the core of our Christian faith is a commitment to work on behalf of and with those marginalized by our society—the hungry, sick, poor, prisoners, strangers, and powerless (Matt. 25:44), those who, day after day, are faced with injustices in our neighborhoods and communities.

Until I was faced with the most horrific thing a person could endure, I lived in my own little bubble, trying to be a good Christian and following the Ten Commandments. I had a gratifying ministry of chaplaincy. Then, tragedy struck and my world turned upside down. Not only did the families and the city of Charleston mourn, the world mourned with us. We found ourselves asking why and how this could happen. All of a sudden decisions had to made about funerals. The media was invading our homes, workplaces, and houses of worship. Families were divided, with different factions claiming power and authority to make decisions without the consensus of all.

During those days, I was in a whirlwind—trying to hold on, screaming inside all the while! I and others struggled on so many levels. Suddenly, we all were faced with issues we'd never considered. I was faced with deeper theological considerations than I had dared to ponder before. We, as a group, and I personally, faced issues of racism, gun violence, the death penalty, and forgiveness.

---

1 "Church must 'speak and live in truth' to combat racism, bishop says," Feb. 1, 2018, *The Catholic Miscellany,* themiscellany.org.

I had to rethink every Scripture passage I had read, and I prayed harder than I ever had before. I was mourning my mother and grieving the loss of eight others—all in the public eye. I was like a zombie. I looked somewhat normal, but inside I was numb and hollow. I had to discover a new way of being in this world, and a new ministry.

My main message is this: Gun violence and racism affect everybody, on every level. As people who say we believe the Holy Scriptures, our actions are anything but caring toward the least of these. Our moral compass is broken, and the direction of our nation's soul is stretched between what political party we identify with.

Having commonsense gun laws is a moral issue. This is about living together in community. This is about caring for all people because God created us all. This is about the sanctity of life—every life. We can't pick and choose which lives are most important. Each of us is worth protecting, and all of us deserve the right to be safe and secure in our homes, our schools, our places of worship, and our places of recreation.

Many people are trying to determine what should be the role of clergy in talking about political issues. The question is often asked of me: "Gun violence and gun rights are clearly political issues, but are they also more than that?"

This is absolutely political, but I'm not sure how clergy are supposed to not be political when it's the world in which we live. It is our job as clergy and leaders to help our congregations think critically about gun violence and racism.

Even in the Bible, our sacred texts are political. From Genesis, God's people are about trying to figure out life as people of faith interacting with the world. When we look at the gospels...well, if Jesus wasn't political, I don't know who was. When he said, "The kingdom is at hand" in the middle of the Roman Empire, this was a political statement! That was a statement about Jesus' kingdom, *and* about the literal kingdom of the empire. Turning over the money exchangers' tables in the temple, dining with prostitutes and tax collectors, and speaking truth to power—all of that was political.

The Gospel itself is political. It's just a matter of our willingness to read it that way, even down to the crucifixion of Jesus, which was capital punishment. Jesus was executed by the government for political reasons.

One approach for clergy to help change the trajectory is taking the long-term perspective in preaching and teaching. Change does not happen overnight, so I always ask preachers, "What are the hopes for your ministry over the long term?"

Every congregation is shaped by what it hears over time. This is how we develop our values. The ongoing narrative that comes from the pulpit and the Christian education ministry shapes the values of the congregation and yields long-term change. To quote Chinese philosopher Lao Tzu: "A journey of a thousand miles must begin with a single step."

Additionally, since we clergy say we value life, we need to consider how we preach that value over the long term in our congregations and contexts—and not just how we value the lives of people who look like us, or think like us, or worship like we do. If we truly value life, we must preach the worth of all life.

A third way to think about ministry is this: "How do we teach in the midst of resistance?" In preaching and teaching on anything—even the topics preachers may think are absolutely "safe"—clergy will meet with resistance to the message.

If the message is given within a congregational context that says, "It's my right to own my shotgun or my pistol or my M16," then you have to find a way to talk so the other person can hear you.

"Okay, fine. It's your right to own it. I get that. But what do you think about background checks? What do you know about loophole laws? Should convicted murderers have the same right to own a gun as you?"

I believe preachers can find something their listeners can agree with and some common ground to begin the conversation. If the sermon gets people on board to say, "Yes, we value life and God values life, so we have a responsibility to take care of life and to take care of one another," then you may be able to introduce the Charleston murders and their impact.

"Well, look at this tragedy. During Bible study in a historic black church, nine people were killed because of the color of their skin." That statement addresses gun violence and racism. Or you might say, "Let's look at what happened in Newtown, Connecticut, when a mentally ill young man murdered twenty children and six adults at Sandy Hook Elementary." That message addresses gun laws and mental illness.

Clergy have to figure out how to create parallels for people who are resistant to the message. What can they *not* disagree with? If we can get them to say, "Yes, I can't disagree with that," then by the time we get around to the tough issue that is really the same thing, they'll also say, "Oh, yeah."

In teaching these tough topics, those of us who possess education and knowledge around texts know there are plenty of interpretations we can extract from any Scripture we decide to preach. At the same time, we must consider, "How do I do the least harm even as I tackle these tough topics?" We're not just tackling a text. We're tackling a text that has authority in the community and the community's way of life. Nevertheless, it's important not to be abrasive and block any possibility of people hearing the message.

Every church and every pastor must decide how to faithfully address the dual issues of racism and gun violence in our country. The Charleston shootings pushed me into the public eye, but it's not a route I would wish on anybody. Every person who has lost a loved one to gun violence is part of that club nobody wants to be in. You learn to deal with it, but it's always right there. You never get over it.

My job is to get to people's hearts. That's where the change has to come—and that's where the church comes in. It's our job as clergy to use the Holy Scriptures and the message of God to lead hearts. In this way, we will do more good than we could ever do harm.

If we could get to people's hearts and move them toward willingness to take action, we could, at last, work toward building the Beloved Community Dr. King talked about.

Some people have asserted that if the Sandy Hook Elementary School killings didn't persuade people that we need better gun laws, then nothing will. Twenty little children slaughtered at school should be enough to soften anyone's heart. But there are a lot of hard hearts out there.

It is so very discouraging to hear people put the right to bear arms above the right those children had to grow up. Sandy Hook only started the conversation. There is so much more to do, and many more hearts to touch. And that's the role clergy has to play—continue to push our members to have the hard conversations, to think deeply about the sacredness of life, to educate themselves about the gun laws in their states, and to become active in our democracy.

This is a heavy subject for church leaders. How do you talk about the issues that we have to deal with as a society on an everyday level? A lot of people may not to want to go there, but we have to.

We live in the world. We don't live in the church. And sometimes, the world comes crashing into the church in violent, terrible ways. So leaders have to find creative, thought-provoking ways of getting the message to the people in their churches. We can't just sit by and watch the outside world, saying, "We don't have to be a part of that."

Church leaders have to be messengers and contextualize societal issues from a spiritual perspective. Our job is to help congregants understand ways that we can be the people who God has called us to be, and not walk in fear.

The world isn't all "Kumbaya," so as leaders, we can't let our churches be simply warm and fuzzy places that then release our members into a brutal world. Certainly, the Charleston massacre and other church mass shootings prove that, inevitably, the world will come crashing into the church.

So we must continue to do what we do because evil shows up *everywhere*—in churches and schools and nightclubs and movie theaters—and we're a part of the everywhere. So if our faith is in God, then we don't walk in fear. All we can do is try to preach the message of love.

Since the Emanuel shootings, I've been to events where there were security guards and officers stationed for my protection. It had never dawned on me before that I could start talking about gun violence and somebody would kill me because they didn't like what I had to say.

Nevertheless, I don't walk in fear. All I can do is preach the message of love.

CHAPTER 12

A Long Road to Forgiveness

Anyone who has lost a loved one to violence—whether in a mass shooting or in an everyday murder—never gets over it. I have heard and sat with mothers, fathers, aunts, uncles, sisters, and brothers who have lost a loved one to gun violence. Listening to mothers, especially, talk about the pain of losing a child, you realize that it's not something you ever get over. You learn to deal with it, but it's always there.

My journey toward forgiveness has been hard, lonely, and complicated.

Immediately after the tragedy, national attention was given to how great it was that the families extended forgiveness to a monster. That tone was set forty-eight hours after the murders at Dylann Roof's court arraignment. My sister, Nadine Collier, was the first person to speak at that hearing.

"I forgive you," she told him.

I was watching the national news from Dallas as the sound bite of forgiveness was publicized all over the world. I was shocked. Hell, I was more than shocked. I was angry! *How could this be? Forgive him? Who has had time to even digest what just happened?*

What a story for the media! So inspirational, these black folks forgiving a white supremacist murderer. You never heard anyone on the news after the mass shootings at Sandy Hook Elementary, the Aurora movie theater, Orlando's Pulse Nightclub, or near Mandalay Bay in Las Vegas forgiving the man who slaughtered their loved ones. You didn't hear anyone talking about forgiveness after *those* shootings.

Nobody was talking about forgiveness right after those shootings. Instead, everybody was sending "thoughts and prayers." *Really? Are you really praying? And if so, good. And what else are you doing?*

But the tone was set. Church members who had just lost loved ones displayed such grace and dignity after the murders. Charleston was pegged as a place with such amazing grace.

I disagreed with Nadine. I had not forgiven Dylann Roof, but I respected my sister's position. She had a right to her own emotions and grieving process. But after the shooting, several articles came out that exploited our various ways of grieving. They pitted us against each other in ways I couldn't understand. That really angered me.

For example, in a cover story after the shootings, *TIME* magazine reported on Nadine's forgiveness speech:

> ..."I forgive you." Those three words reverberated through the courtroom and across the cable wires, down the fiber-optic lines, carried by invisible storms of ones and zeros that fill the air from cell tower to cell tower and magically cohere in the palms of our hands. They took the world by surprise.
>
> They took Collier's own family by surprise. "When she said that, I was just shocked," says [Sharon] Risher. "I was like, Who in the hell is she talking for? Because she's not talking for me."...
>
> Risher was not the only person who felt that her sister's words were premature. After [Nadine] Collier spoke, says Risher, others felt pressure to echo her words. "I'm a reverend. I'm in the church," Risher notes, a bit defensively. "And I understand that forgiveness is a process. Some people with their beliefs can automatically forgive, but I'm not there yet. And I know that God is not going to look at me any different because I have not forgiven Dylann Roof yet."
>
> The tense feelings were exacerbated in the days and weeks that followed, as Collier's face appeared on nearly every news program and donations poured in to Emanuel from around the world and talk started of books and movies and maybe even a Nobel Peace Prize. The publicity drove a wedge between the children of Ethel Lance. "My sister Esther and I have been pushed aside, and everybody has gathered around Nadine," Risher says.
>
> Instead of siblings being a comfort to each other, they've stopped speaking. Tragedy does not always bring people closer; some earthquakes leave nothing but rubble. "From my understanding, my family is not the only family in turmoil," Risher says.[1]

1   David von Drehle, with Jay Newton-Small and Maya Rhodan, "How Do You Forgive a Murder?" Nov. 23, 2015, *TIME*, http://Time.Com/Time-Magazine-Charleston-Shooting-Cover-Story/.

On September 10, 2015, I went with some representatives from Everytown to do a CNN interview with Brooke Baldwin. This was during the time when I was saying, "I don't forgive him yet." I felt like they wanted me to go along with everybody else and say I had forgiven the killer. But my mind was made up. *You know what? No. I'm not gonna say that. I don't care who else said it, even Nadine. This is now how I feel, and I'm just not gonna go along with it.*

I stuck to my resolve, but still I felt judged. A lot of that came from being a person of the cloth. People think that clergy are supposed to automatically forgive and be perfect. But what I was saying was a true reflection of how I felt, and I just wasn't gonna back down.

Three months after Momma's death, I spoke to a crowd in front of the Washington Monument: "It's time to rise, people. To rise from Chattanooga, to rise from Lafayette, to rise from Roanoke, to rise for the awful number of Americans who are killed by gun violence" (longer excerpt from this speech in in chapter 8).

And here is what *The Trace,* which covers gun-related news, reported about my message that day:

> At the memorial service to honor Risher's murdered relatives, President Obama dipped his head and sang "Amazing Grace." Other family members of the Emanuel nine were praised for their humility and grace when they stood at the accused gunman's arraignment and forgave him through agonized sobs. Tears, somber remembrances, and candlelit vigils usually define the public's reaction to a high-profile shooting; anger is less commonly broadcast on cable news, which is why Risher's indignation was so striking. She is not ready for absolution, and she's unabashed about the axe she still carries three months after the attack.
>
> After expending some of her anger on Roof, Risher, who is a trauma chaplain at Parkland Hospital in Texas and sees gunshot wounds every day, unloaded on the lawmakers across the street.
>
> As the event drew to a close and the field before the podium cleared of people... Risher was found sitting unaccompanied on a bench, gazing into the sunny afternoon. She rested her leg on her scooter, and offered a final thought on forgiveness.
>
> "I'm just not there yet," she told me. "You're gonna forgive somebody who doesn't even wanna be forgiven?

Forgiveness is about you moving on. So I don't even think about this little punk."[2]

That's some heavy judgment from a person who has no idea what it's like the endure what I'd gone through.

I finally decided there comes a time when we have to stand for what believe and stay in that space for however long it takes. I had to feel what I felt and keep it moving. I was not going to just hop onto the forgiveness bandwagon simply because someone else thought that I should.

Then I was at church one Sunday in Charlotte. The music was awesome and the preacher was on a roll. He started to talk about forgiveness. He told the congregation that forgiveness should be instant and is not a process, because God wants us to forgive instantly. My heart almost leaped out of my chest. I couldn't believe what I was hearing. What about the people like me who are struggling to get there? What about helping us get there? Helping us know that it's okay to work through such a heavy spiritual act?

I want others to know this: You can empower yourself to speak your truth. You are allowed to articulate how you truly feel. You can allow yourself to go through the process and then perform whatever acts you have to do to forgive. In my heart of hearts, I knew forgiveness would come for me at some point. I understood even then that forgiveness is one of the hallmarks of the Christian faith. I had to work hard spiritually to walk toward forgiveness. I guess I just didn't want to let go of the deep anger because the grief and pain were so intense. Yet, I never stopped praying—and, I never stopped yelling at God.

I allowed myself the time it took. I don't feel like I'm any worse because I didn't forgive this man instantly. I haven't found a scripture that lays out how much time it takes, or how much time God allows us to forgive. I knew I would get there someday—because, as a Christian, I have no other choice.

A year after Momma's murder, I did an interview with *Voices,* an online publication of an organization called Death Penalty Focus. The struggle in my heart comes through in what I said:

> ..."I'm not in the same emotional space where I was a year ago...a lot of the anger and bitterness has subsided. It's tempered now and my heart is still wanting to get there. But

2 Jennifer Mascia, "Thunder on the Mall, a Charleston Victim's Daughter Takes Her Message to Washington," Sept. 12, 2015, The Trace, https://www.thetrace.org/2015/09/washington-rally-charleston-risher-gun-violence/).

I'm not there yet. It just seems so hard to be able to forgive someone who planned that whole thing."

Risher has moved to North Carolina to be near her son and daughter who live there. More than a year after her mother and cousins died, her grief is still raw. "Some days I don't even want to get out of bed. Every step you take forward in healing, something happens that throws you right back," she says. "I belong to the loneliest club, a club nobody wants to be a member of."[3]

A few weeks after that interview, a seminary buddy, Mark Hinchcliff, invited me to Martinsville, Virginia, to preach for a World Communion interfaith service there. Mark is pastor of First Presbyterian Church in Martinsville, a city that has a history strongly rooted in the Confederacy. We drove by places where the Confederate flag was still flying.

The interfaith service included many different denominations. As I was preaching, I started to say something about forgiveness. In talking about forgiveness, I felt a whisper of warmth come over me. God was telling me, "Okay, it's time for you to go ahead and say you forgive Dylann Roof. You've done did all the work. You've gotten past all of this. You can go ahead and say it now."

And that's what I did. That was the first time I actually said that I forgave Dylann Roof.

I'd never planned to just say it publicly, because I'd always thought that was something between me and God. But in the midst of preaching that sermon, I publicly forgave my mother's murderer.

I started crying up a storm. I kept my composure as much as I could, but the tears kept rolling down my face because I had wrestled with that so much. Maybe a lot of that had to do with me just not wanting to forgive the man who took my mother's life. But on the other hand, since I'm called to be a minister, I know that I'm also called to bring some hope to people. I have to be the best person I can be. It was time for me to forgive.

God gave me the time I needed. "Hey, Sharon, I'm gonna let you do what you do. I'm gonna let you just go ahead with all of the feelings that you have, because I know that you're mine. And eventually, you'll come to where you need to be with that. And when it happens, it will be for real. It's not gonna be something you'll ever go back and say, 'I wish I'd never said that.' Because, if you take the time to work it

---

3 "Voices—Sharon Risher," Death Penalty Focus blog, deathpenalty.org/blog/the-focus/abolitionist-month-sharon-risher/ .

through, then it's settled. You're my child, and—just like I can forgive you and everybody else, because I got up on that cross and died—you can do this."

I also knew that Momma would want me to forgive, because she would always say, "I've done some things that I'm not proud of. Lots of things. But the more I keep trying to please Jesus, the better off I know my life is." Momma always believed that if something caused a stumbling block to Jesus, then you needed to figure it out.

I talk to Momma all the time, though. All the time. While I'm sitting on the patio, surrounded by plants and drinking coffee, I'll be like, "Yeah, Momma, I know. Yeah, I know." For most of my adult life, I didn't live in the same city as my momma, but our spiritual connection transcended the miles.

Sometimes I'll be cooking, or if I clean the kitchen and I don't sweep the floor, I can hear her saying, "The kitchen's not clean until the floor is swept."

And I'll look at the floor, like, "Yeah, Momma. Not today."

Aja and I always talk about her. My daughter really knows how to talk in the Charleston brogue. Charlestonians, especially blacks, have a Southern drawl mixed with the Gullah language. Aja knows to mimic that perfectly. Sometimes when we're together and she'll start talking like Momma or Esther or Nadine. That's how we keep Momma alive.

Momma's always around because the things she instilled in us are still with us. When we were kids, and even as adults, we could never do anything to suit her standards. Momma would never allow us to wear wrinkled clothes. We always had to be neat, pressed, and well dressed. So now, if Aja puts on something wrinkled, I may look at her and say, "Now you know your grandma is turning around in her grave right now, with you in that wrinkled shirt." So Momma will always be around us to make sure we do things right.

I still miss her terribly, but there is a calmness in my soul about Momma. I know she is all right.

* * * * *

God has been good to me, but these last couple years I have been hurled into the fiery furnace. I stepped out in faith and resigned my position as a chaplain. I moved back to Charlotte with no idea how I would make enough money to support myself.

That's the scary part, as well as the good part, of believing in God. I wonder, sometimes, *Will I be able to continue to do these speaking engagements?* Because right now that's my only income. *Will I have to go back to being a chaplain?* I don't know. I have no plan, and that's scary. But I just keep saying, "Okay, God, I don't need anything."

Brandon and Aja have taken care of me. I can't tell you how it feels to know that your children have your back and you don't have to worry. I'm blessed, and I know it. I've got a little money in the bank; not a lot, but some. I've been trying to hold onto my pennies. Now, I feel like it's finally time for me to leave the security of Aja's house; it has been my security blanket.

It's time for me to get back out there and be Sharon. But, well, *which* Sharon? I'll wonder: *What am I gonna do? Am I gonna get out there and get an apartment and live on my own? Can I afford it?* And then I think about God telling me: *Why are you worrying about this? Haven't I taken care of you?*

This faith thing is scary, but there's a peace that comes with that scariness. For the first time in my life, I don't know what the hell I'm doing next, and I'm peaceful.

And if anybody thinks living by faith is not the hardest thing you'll ever do, they're wrong! I up and quit my job like I knew what the hell I was doing! And that was because of the faith I had in God. I knew what I was doing was right; still, it was hard and it was scary. It still is, but I'm God's child, and He knows I'm gonna get it right eventually.

God is working things out for me to carry the message that God says, "I will provide for you. I always have, even when you didn't even pay attention to me. I've always been there, and I'm gonna be there always."

So I'm still trying to figure out what God plans for me. I just can't quite see my path, so I'm just going to continue walking step by step as God lays it out before me. I am speaking at colleges and universities all over the country, and I've been preaching in churches. That, and my advocacy work, have kept me busy.

Dr. King said, "Nothing will be done until people of good will put their bodies and their souls in motion. And it will be the kind of soul force brought into being as a result of this confrontation that I believe will make the difference."[4]

All of us will face some challenges in life, and how we press forward will define who we will become. I didn't ask for this journey. I would rather not be a survivor of gun violence. I'd give anything in the world

---

4 Martin Luther King Jr., "Remaining Awake Through a Great Revolution," sermon delivered at the National Cathedral in Washington, D.C. on March 31, 1968, https://kinginstitute.stanford.edu/king-papers/publications/knock-midnight-inspiration-great-sermons-reverend-martin-luther-king-jr-10 .

to turn back time, to prevent the shooting, and to have my mother here with me.

But here I am.

I stand in solidarity with Lucy McBath (who is now a member of the United States House of Representatives from Georgia's sixth congressional district), Everytown for Gun Safety, and Moms Demand Action for Gun Sense in America. I stand in solidarity with the young people who have arisen in the wake of the Stoneman Douglas High School shootings in Parkland, Florida. I am *so* inspired by those young people! A mass shooting threw them into a national debate, just like me. They didn't ask for it, and never would have wanted it, but they are rising to the call. They know they should not have to be afraid of getting shot at school.

David Hogg has become a passionate young advocate for sensible gun laws, and Emma Gonzáles is just fierce. When I met her in the summer of 2018, we hugged a *long* time. She said, "You give the best hugs!" I admire her fierceness. Bria Smith is another articulate and passionate teenager from Milwaukee, where her neighborhood has been plagued by gun violence.

I am inspired by the passion of these young people. They are not going to shut up and they are not going to back down. They are registering to vote, so they are a force that America is gonna have to reckon with. I believe Moms Demand, Everytown, and March for Our Lives are just the tip of the iceberg. Millions of Americans want sensible gun laws. In fact, a Gallup poll conducted Oct. 5–11, 2017, just days after the Las Vegas shooting, showed that 95 percent of those surveyed favored universal background checks, 75 percent favored a thirty-day waiting period for all gun sales, and 70 percent favored requiring all privately owned guns to be registered with the police.[5] A year later, an October 2018 poll showed that sixty-one percent favored stricter laws on the sale of firearms.

A lot of things need to be worked out. We simply have to come to an agreement on what sensible gun laws look like, but people are beginning to see that we cannot just let things go on as they are. We can't just accept mass shooting after mass shooting, month after month.

Whenever a mass shooting happens, it makes the news for a little while, and then the media moves on to the next cycle. I feel my life's

---

5 Lydia Saad, "Americans Widely Support Tighter Regulations on Gun Sales," Oct. 17, 2017, gallup.com news, https://news.gallup.com/poll/220637/americans-widely-support-tighter-regulations-gun-sales.aspx.

calling now is to always remind people about the *why* of what happened in that church and *how* we have to continue trying make things better. So as long as people want to listen to me, I'm gonna be there. I don't ever want those nine lives to be forgotten.

The tide is changing. And I'm proud to be a part of that tidal change. I am proud of my new ministry. I know Momma would be proud of me. And I am so proud to be her daughter.

On June 17, 2015, a twenty-one-year old white man went to Emanuel African Methodist Episcopal Church and murdered as many people as he could. He had done months of research and preparation, including several road trips to Charleston from Columbia, South Carolina. He plotted his route to and from the church.

On that day, members of my family and others were attending their regular Wednesday night Bible study. Earlier that evening, the church had been packed full of people attending the general conference meeting of that District of the AME church. Because the meeting ran into the time for Bible study, a discussion was held whether to cancel.

The faithful stayed to study the Word. They welcomed this young man into the church and sat him near the pastor. After about an hour of studying the Gospel of Mark, chapter 4, they gathered in a circle and held hands for the prayer of dismissal. With their heads bowed and their eyes closed, their lives came to a fateful end.

He slaughtered them while they were praying. He robbed the Charleston community of nine lives and afflicted an entire community because he hated their skin color. The five people who survived must live with the horrific memories of that tragedy every day.

I continue to say the names of those lost because my mission in life is helping other people know that hate won't win.

I continue to call each name because they gave their lives for a higher purpose and they should always be remembered: my mother, Mrs. Ethel Lee Lance; my two cousins, Mrs. Susie Jackson, who was eighty-seven years old, and Tywanza Sanders, who was twenty-six; a childhood friend, Myra Thompson; the pastor of the church, Rev. Clementa C. Pinckney; Rev. Daniel Simmons; Rev. Sharonda Coleman-Singleton; Mrs. Cynthia Marie Graham Hurd; and Rev. Depayne Middleton-Doctor.

I pray that whenever you hear their names, you feel empowered to help invoke change.

Lessons Learned

Life has given me challenges and failures, good times and bad times. Along my journey I have known feelings of hopelessness, shame, guilt, and unworthiness. Sometimes I have replayed old tapes of toxicity in my mind and plunged into darkness, wallowing in all things negative. Yet, inside I knew, *Sharon, you're better than this*, and that eventually I would find my way back to the present.

But life has given me some lessons that I want to share with anyone willing to take heed. My stuff may not compare to someone else's, but we all have stuff. No matter who you are, what you have, the house you live in, the job or title you hold, life is going to toss you around sometimes. Nevertheless, God has given us all what we need to be the best person we can be.

The things to ask yourself are, "Am I comfortable with who I am? Can I be content being the authentic me? Is there room for change in my life? Am I willing to do some deep self-reflection and take inventory of myself? Is there purpose in my life beyond just getting through?"

Sometimes I sought answers to those questions, and at other times life forced me to reckon with the solutions. Consequently, I have learned a few things along this journey called my life.

You can't heal in isolation. This is one of the first things I learned after the Emanuel tragedy. After the shootings, planning Momma's funeral, and attending Rev. Pinckney's service, I returned to Dallas, where I was alone with my thoughts twenty-four hours a day. For weeks I allowed myself to wallow in my pain and grief. I couldn't process everything that had happened. I didn't call anyone except my children and Esther.

Even my conversations with my children mostly consisted of automatic responses to their questions about how I was doing. Caring for my beloved pet gave me a reason to keep going. Puff Daddy is old and needs medication and care beyond the normal walking and potty times. So I had to get up.

People were calling at times to check on me, but I still felt alone and lost. When I returned to work at the hospital, so many of the nurses and even some of the doctors stopped me to express their heartfelt condolences. All of this was going on in the midst of the hospital's move across the street to a new billion-dollar facility.

My ankle was hurting a lot, but it was nothing compared to the emotional pain I was experiencing. I made it through on autopilot. I was grieving the loss of my mother and the transition from a place now called Old Parkland. I had invested so much of myself in that place, where I was respected among my colleagues. I had loved being with the patients there and felt that I was finally in my dream job. Maybe it was just too much change during a time when my foundation had been pulled from underneath me. My heart was just not ready to move on and I had a severely broken ankle, so I took medical leave from the hospital. I was all alone in Dallas, and now with medical needs.

I was miserable. Finally, I decided to come out of the darkness and reach out to people—to reach out myself. Maybe people just didn't know what to say, and so, sometimes, they said nothing. The why was unimportant. All I knew was that I had to reach out for help, so I began making calls. In reaching out I discovered that the people in my life who loved me were there for me, and I really needed them.

The first person who changed things for me was Lucy McBath from Everytown. When she reached out to me, it felt like finally somebody knew what I was going through. As a hospital chaplain, I had met families who'd lost loved ones to violence and were dealing with that kind of grief. But I was in counselor mode then. Lucy asked me how *I* felt. It was so easy to talk to her. I could just let her see my grief. I didn't have to protect her from it. She allowed me to cry, which was a gift. And she cried with me. That was special. Everyone needs that. I knew it was okay, because Lucy had been through what I was going through. I could be real with Lucy.

Michael Waters came into my life at a point when I had stopped going to church. I didn't want people to be uncomfortable around me because they didn't know what to say. I found church services on the Web. I had met Michael before and started watching his church's live stream services on my computer. Eventually, I made up my mind to visit his church. During all of this time, I was dealing with my broken ankle. I couldn't walk and couldn't drive, but I found a way to start going to his church.

From that first visit to his church, Michael became my pastor. People always say, "If you ever need anything, call me." Well, he said that, and he meant that. Just like with Lucy, it was a connection of knowing in my gut that he was sincere. So I would call Michael when I was crying or sad or angry, and he would listen to me. He wasn't preachy or throwing scriptures at me. He just let me cry. He let me talk, and he would always tell me, "We are here for you. The church is here for you. If there is anything we can do, please let us do."

I felt like he was my personal pastor. He ministered to me. It wasn't about a congregation. It was just to me as a person. And I thank God for that.

God had placed good people to help me. I just needed the sense to know that I needed help. All I had to do was ask, and help was there.

Trust your gut instinct and cling to your faith. Instinct is knowing deep in the pit of your stomach, or even your soul, what is the right thing to do. Sometimes we make selfish decisions. Whether it's a personal decision or a financial one, when we act solely from selfishness, we know deep inside it's not the right thing to do. So we give ourselves justification for our choices and end up making bad decisions and living with the consequences.

Sometimes our selfish choices have a severe impact on others. We cause pain to our loved ones with our bad decisions. When I provoked Bernard into the fight that led to our separation, I knew that I was wrong. But I kept making justifications for what I'd done. I ignored my gut instinct, and I caused so much pain, especially to my children.

But I have always felt okay about my decisions when I trusted my instinct and my faith, even though sometimes it's scary. When I came back to Dallas after the shootings, and was on medical leave for a while, my boss called several times to find out when I was coming back and all of that. At the same time, I was grieving the move from of the old building, which had become a home to me. The old Parkland Hospital felt secure, safe.

While on leave, I already had some worries about whether I could go back and engage in the ministry I so dearly loved. Momma's death had changed me, and my soul was saying, "I'm not gonna be able to do it."

During that last phone call when my boss asked when I was coming back, my gut instinct confirmed, "You're not going back."

I have second-guessed that decision a lot. There is always that craving for the old normal. I liked having work to do—knowing my schedule, knowing that I would be helping people at the hospital. I enjoyed my work. Mostly, my tendency to reevaluate my decision to leave Parkland is just me wanting my old life back.

In my mind, trusting your gut instinct is really about clinging to your faith. It is knowing that, no matter what happens, God's with you. As my savings dwindle and speaking engagements come farther apart, I keep affirming, "Okay, God, I'm not going to worry about money. You've taken me this far. I'm not gonna worry."

My gut instinct tells me it's going to be all right because I'm doing what I'm supposed to do. If I get down to five dollars in my bank account, I still know it's going to be all right because God hasn't failed me yet.

I'm not saying the prosperity preachers are right when they say, "Oh, if you believe, God will make you rich." There have been times in my life when I felt like I was in the ocean and about to drown. The water was getting ready to go in my damn nose. That's the way it has felt for me to be patient and wait on God. But I know that water will not drown me. I will come out of it.

That's what it means to trust your God-directed instincts and go with what you know is right. It was really hard to leave my kids in North Carolina and move to Dallas to attend seminary, but my gut said they would be all right. God told me, "Yes, you have to do all of this." So I left, trusting my gut and my faith no matter how hard it was.

Be prepared to get rejected. In life, there will be times when you're told, "No." That's just the bottom line. How we deal with that rejection tells how we will continue to move forward. If you're going stay down every time somebody tells you no, you're not gonna make it.

And truthfully, sometimes getting a *no* is a good thing. If I had gotten everything I wanted in life, I don't know if I'd even be alive today. I think about things I wanted that were not good for me, and somehow or another they didn't work out. I can look back and say, "That was the best thing that could have happened." Sometimes getting a *no* positions us to do greater things.

Growing up, I was the light-skinned girl with the curly hair in a neighborhood of dark-skinned people. I had a few good friends, such as Myra Thompson, but I faced a lot of rejection. Some people tried to bully me, but I just didn't let them. My momma was a fighter and she taught her children to be fighters. So, you throw me down, I get back up.

One of the toughest rejections I ever faced was the one that forced me to leave the Presbyterian Church. I had attended seminary mostly on the Presbyterian Church's dime, but to get ordained in the Presbyterian Church candidates have to pass five written exams. Well, I passed two or three of them and couldn't pass the rest. My committee in North Carolina kept wanting me to take the exams over, and I did. I took them three times, but I just couldn't do it.

I felt like the Presbyterian Church could have worked with me, as they already had a lack of people of color in the denomination. I had graduated from their seminary, and they couldn't figure out a way to have me ordained? That hurt. That rejection was heart-wounding on a whole different level.

Since ordination was off the table, I had to make a decision about whether I was going to let this defeat me or whether I was going to pursue other options. *Well, God made more than the Presbyterian Church.*

During my hospital chaplaincy, my friend Pam Jones from the VA hospital invited me to attend World Harvest Church, which is nondenominational. "Come to church with me. I think our bishop will like you. You've got your degree, and you could probably do some good things with our church."

I went with her, and soon started working with the church's food pantry. World Harvest ordained me, and that ordination gave me what I needed to continue my chaplaincy training. Because of my faith, and because of my momma, I found another way.

You've got to persevere. No matter what, you have to keep trying. That is something I learned from Momma. Something in her said that no matter what life threw at you, you still have to figure out how to survive. She had five kids that she needed to take care of. When I was young, Momma did laundry and ironing for a white lady named Miss Anne. I remember going with her and watching her work.

Later, when Momma worked at the auditorium, she sometimes took me with her, and I would help her clean up. She was a hard worker. When she finished cleaning, you would know that Ethel had been there, because everything was done right.

After Momma was killed, during the times when I felt like giving up, I could hear her saying, "What you gonna do? Fold up?"

And always there was that knowing: *Yeah, you might be down for a little while, but you're not down for the count. You just can't give up, no matter what.*

When I think about my family and what my ancestors survived, it motivates me. In my head I know I'm biracial, but in my heart I'm black. Blackness isn't just about skin color; blackness is about our souls. Our black souls came from across the water and survived the Middle Passage, slavery, Jim Crow, and denied opportunities. If they survived all of that, who am I not to be the best I can be?

Don't give up on humanity. If you give up on humanity, what are you going to do? Lock yourself up in your house and not be a part of society? You can't give up.

My friend Arno is a former a white supremacist. When we met, I really didn't believe that someone could change that much. Even though Arno doesn't share my faith tradition, I had to realize that, in my own faith, Jesus Christ can change anybody. And I had to accept Arno, because I know that God changed me too. You just can't say that people can't change, because we already know the changing power of God.

In my speaking across the country, my faith in humanity is restored. After I speak, people offer condolences and hug me, and often we pray together. All of that reaffirms that—whether black, brown, red, yellow, or white—there are a lot of good people in the world.

You have to take care of yourself. Nurture your body and your soul.

At sixty years old, I'm finally able to pay attention to me. I have abused this body in more ways than one. I've had some issues with my knees, a hysterectomy, and a few mammogram scares, but basically, I'm in decent health. I take my vitamins. I have arthritis and sciatica, but all in all, I'm good. I might make it another twenty-five years.

But just as important as taking care of your body, you have to take care of your soul. I believe in the power of laughter. You have to be able to laugh at yourself.

I have done many things that were so funny I had to laugh at myself. I'm clumsy and I will just trip while walking. Sometimes, I'll lose my glasses, only to find them right where I left them. I have to laugh at myself for that. With everything going on in the world, laughter at such moments is a great release.

I was in New York City last year and I had a meeting at Bloomberg Tower. I didn't check the address. I just called an Uber. And the driver picked me up, drove one block, and said, "Ma'am, you're at your destination."

I looked back, and I could see the hotel! I just sat there and burst out laughing. I'd just assumed that because I was in New York, I was going a great distance. That one-block ride cost me a few dollars, but gave me a great big laugh in return.

We can't be heavy all the time. We're all into our jobs, raising kids, and whatever it is we are doing. We have to release stress. Whatever we're doing, we have to just be able to laugh at ourselves.

Another way that I take care of myself is though music. It's healing to me, and I have music for my every mood. I take the message and use it as a mantra.

Kendrick Lamar's "Alright" came out around the time of the Charleston shootings. There is anger and pain and all of that in his lyrics—accompanied by a funky beat. Over and over he says, "But we gon' be alright." That song gave me a way to dance and feel and know I wasn't the only one who'd felt anger and pain. I can put myself in that song. Esther was the same way. That was our song. We'd say, "We gon' be alright," because everything was so heavy.

Drake's "Started from the Bottom" is another song I can relate to, because I've felt that I started from the bottom. His song gives hope that you can start from the bottom, and still go places. I never in my life thought that someday I would be flying around this country and people would actually want to hear me speak.

Those songs uplifted me, even when my circumstances were heavy and my hope was dim.

Music always has been part of my life, and dancing was a part of our family. I grew up with Smokey Robinson and Diana Ross, and all of that great music. We all listened to the radio and we danced. I rely on the old hymns too, as they are part of our family tradition. Even before Momma joined Emanuel, she played gospel music. Saturdays were gospel music days, and we listened to that music while we did our Saturday chores.

Music and laughter are as important as vitamins and medical checkups. They will heal your soul.

Everybody has a purpose. Now that I'm in my seventh decade, I finally believe that I'm where I'm supposed to be, and that I'm operating in my purpose—advocating for sensible gun laws and speaking about racism, and Momma, and my own experiences.

Each of us has a purpose, so we need to live purposeful lives. We need to be nice and kind and talk to people who don't look like us. Maybe your one purpose today is to open a door for an old lady who needs you right at that moment. Your purpose is to be the best you that God has equipped you to be. And if you're a person of faith, you'll try and live by the moral compass of your faith and what you believe.

I believe that if we follow the Ten Commandments we're on the right track. If we do what God has called us to do as His people, we will be all right. And when we slip, then we confess. "Here I am God, messing up again. So that same grace and mercy you gave me last week, can I have some more?" I joke about it, but I know that grace is for real.

If you try to do the right thing, if you try to be loving and kind, then you'll be all right.

Use the wisdom of the role models in your life. The night I heard Dr. Martin Luther King Jr. speak at County Hall, a seed was planted in me. I wanted to be like him. I wanted to speak like him. He inspired me then, and he is still a motivation to me today.

Momma taught me about perseverance. She was my cheerleader. Whatever I got myself into, she was right there to make sure that I could do it. She would see to it that I was going to do it well, and I was gonna look good doing it. Momma always knew presenting yourself well would take you far in life.

When I was young, I wanted to be like Angela Davis. She was out there advocating for black power and talking about the things that we deserve as black people but have to fight for. She said that if fighting is what we need to do, that's just what we need to do. We can't just sit back. That resonated with me because I once had thought I would go to law school and then become a politician, because law is the route often taken to get into politics. Angela Davis was putting it out there, and she looked like me.

So as screwed up as America is, there are people out there we can look up to. Whatever your flavor, you can find somebody to look up to.

You have to put in the work to achieve your dreams. Momma would always say, "You got to get up to find the job. The job ain't gonna find you." That meant you needed to be proactive about achieving what you wanted.

When I was young, I had my life route planned for a career in politics. I knew I'd have to work hard to achieve that, starting with enrolling in college and figuring out how to pay for it. I did work study and I worked at a jewelry store. I did what I had to do to stay in college and work toward what I wanted. I worked hard for that college degree.

In my forties, I followed a new path and enrolled in seminary. Bernard drove me to Dallas, with Brandon and Aja in the back seat. They helped me pack up all my stuff and then they helped me set up my dorm room. We toured the campus, then they hugged and kissed me and said goodbye. After they left, I stood on the dormitory steps, looking over the campus and crying, wondering: *What the hell have I done?*

I got a job in the admissions office and worked harder at my coursework than I have ever done in my life. There were many times when I thought I wouldn't make it through. I took Hebrew three times. I took Greek twice. I hated my Christian history professor with everything I had in my soul because the course required so much memorization. That's not my strength, but I got through it. I would write things down a hundred times, and my hand would get used to what the answers should look like. My apartment had papers everywhere, with Greek and Hebrew taped to the walls. When I got that damned degree, I was so proud because I truly had worked for it.

After graduation, I entered chaplaincy training at the North Texas VA hospital in Dallas. I came up from Austin for the interview in my lucky brown suit. I went through the interview, and before I got back to the front of the hospital to head back to Austin, they called to tell me I had been accepted in the program. Being at the VA hospital meant working with veterans who were dealing with all kinds of trauma and injuries.

My second year of chaplaincy training involved specialized training in mental health and substance abuse. That's when I really started to shine as a teacher. *This is what I'm supposed to be doing. Because, who can talk more about substance abuse than me? I sure know what you're talking about. My experiences might not have been your experiences, but when you're in a fog you're in a fog, no matter what substance it is.* I could relate to the veterans' struggles and come at them from my heart and be real. They had no trouble talking to me because I could relate.

The time God allowed me to attend seminary was the freest I've ever felt in my life, and maybe the most scared, too. I finally had a vision of who I really was and what I could do—again, because of Momma. She taught me the value of working hard and doing your best, and I am so grateful for that. She was there to celebrate my accomplishment at graduation, and she is with me every day as I continue doing my best work.

Through all of the tragedy and hurt, I believe there's a place called heaven, and that my mom is there—with *her* mother, and with Terrie and Esther. When I die, I pray that God then will allow me to enter heaven, too, so I will be reunited with the people that I love. And those spirits, those angels, the saints that have come before me, I believe in the power of their goodness to guide me until that day comes.

About the Authors

Rev. Sharon Risher is a renowned ordained pastor and speaker who has appeared on major media outlets, including CNN, *Good Morning America, CBS News, Roland Martin's News One,* NPR, Guardian-BCC radio, and many others. She has been featured in national and local publications including *TIME, Marie Claire, Essence,* and *Texas Monthly,* among many others. She visited President Obama at the White House on multiple occasions, and has served as a guest speaker for several Martin Luther King Jr. memorial events. She has traveled the country, speaking about her experience of loss, forgiveness, faith, racism, and violence. She is a mother to two grown children, Howard Brandon and Aja Sharnee, and her furry dog-child, Puff Daddy. Visit Risher's website SharonRisherSpeaks.com for more.

Sherri Wood Emmons is an award-winning journalist and the former managing editor of *DisciplesWorld* magazine. She is the author of four novels—*Prayers and Lies* (Kensington Books, 2011), *The Sometimes Daughter* (Kensington Books, 2011), *The Weight of Small Things* (Kensington Books, 2012), and *The Seventh Mother* (Kensington books, 2013)—and the coauthor (with Franklyn Schaefer) of *Defrocked: How a Father's Act of Love Shook the United Methodist Church* (2014, Chalice Press).